From Siblings to Cousins

A FAMILY——
BUSINESS
——PUBLICATION

Family Business Publications are the combined efforts of the Family Business Consulting Group and Palgrave Macmillan. These books provide useful information on a broad range of topics that concern the family business enterprise, including succession planning, communication, strategy and growth, family leadership, and more. The books are written by experts with combined experiences of over a century in the field of family enterprise and who have consulted with thousands of enterprising families the world over, giving the reader practical, effective, and time-tested insights to everyone involved in a family business.

FBCG, founded in 1994, is the leading business consultancy exclusively devoted to helping family enterprises prosper across generations.

FAMILY BUSINESS LEADERSHIP SERIES

This series of books comprises concise guides and thoughtful compendiums to the most pressing issues that anyone involved in a family firm may face. Each volume covers a different topic area and provides the answers to some of the most common and challenging questions.

Titles include:

All of the books were written by members of the Family Business Consulting Group and are based on both our experiences with thousands of client families as well as our empirical research at leading research universities the world over.

From Siblings to Cousins

*Prospering in the Third Generation
and Beyond*

Craig E. Aronoff
and John L. Ward

palgrave
macmillan

First published by the Family Business Consulting Group Publications, 2007.
This edition first published in 2011 by
PALGRAVE MACMILLAN®
in the United States—a division of St. Martin's Press LLC,
175 Fifth Avenue, New York, NY 10010.

Where this book is distributed in the UK, Europe and the rest of the world,
this is by Palgrave Macmillan, a division of Macmillan Publishers Limited,
registered in England, company number 785998, of Houndmills,
Basingstoke, Hampshire RG21 6XS.

Palgrave Macmillan is the global academic imprint of the above companies
and has companies and representatives throughout the world.

Palgrave® and Macmillan® are registered trademarks in the United States,
the United Kingdom, Europe and other countries.

ISBN: 978–0–230–11118–9

Library of Congress Cataloging-in-Publication Data

Aronoff, Craig E.
　　From siblings to cousins : prospering in the third generation and
　beyond / by Craig E. Aronoff and John L. Ward.
　　　p. cm. — (Family business leadership series)
　　Includes bibliographical references and index.
　　Originally published: Marietta, GA : Family Enterprise Publishers,
c2007.
　　　ISBN 978–0–230–11118–9
　　　1. Family-owned business enterprises—Succession. 2. Family-owned
　business enterprises—Management. I. Ward, John L., 1945– II. Title.
HD62.25.A7633 2011
658.1′6—dc22   2010045297

A catalogue record of the book is available from the British Library.

Design by Newgen Imaging Systems (P) Ltd., Chennai, India.

First Palgrave Macmillan edition: January 2011

10 9 8 7 6 5 4 3 2 1

Printed in the United States of America.

Contents

CONTENTS

Exhibits

Chapter 1

Introduction

Your Family's Last Major
Business Transition

Q: What do the New York Times Company, Estée Lauder Companies, Inc., and Highlights for Children, Inc., have in common?

A: They are family businesses that have defied the death sentence promised in that old saying, "Shirtsleeves to shirtsleeves in three generations." They have all survived to become "third tier" businesses—that is, businesses run by the cousin generation. For most family businesses, that's the third generation, although for some businesses, like the New York Times Company, it's the fourth generation or beyond.

While statistics indeed show that most family businesses don't make it to the third generation, these companies and countless others have beaten the odds. Not without difficulty. Not without hard work and thoughtfulness and tough decision making. But they have succeeded at making the last major transition for business-owning families—going from siblings to cousins. It's a transformation your family business can make, too. This book will show you how.

You may wonder why going from siblings to cousins is your family's last major business transformation. Aren't there more transitions to come? Of course there are, but none so complicated as first going from a founder to siblings and then from siblings to cousins. Chapter 2 explains why going from siblings to cousins is so tricky. You will discover that just as the rules changed when your business went from its founder to the sibling generation, so must the rules change again when a cousin generation succeeds the siblings. You will also increase your understanding of what a healthy family business looks like before and after the transition to the cousins takes place.

Family members in businesses that are moving into the cousin stage or who are already in it will gain the most from this book. Family business advisors (attorneys, management consultants, estate planners) can also benefit, perhaps finding ways to assist their clients in making this difficult transition. Others who should find this book useful are family business board members as well as managers of family offices who are working with extended families.

This book is aimed at helping cousins organize themselves and their extended family for success as a group that owns and runs a business together. If you are in the cousin category, it will provide you with a conceptual map that shows you how to think about a cousin-owned business—because a cousin-stage business requires a completely different pattern of thought than a sibling-stage business. You will gain an appreciation for the challenges specific to a cousin business and will learn what it takes to meet those challenges. You will become knowledgeable about the key issues that cousins face, such as how to attract the most capable family members into the business leadership roles or how to develop agreement among owners who may be widely scattered in geography and opinions. You will also find guidelines to help you continue working together successfully—if that's what you choose to do.

From Siblings to Cousins is also addressed to the sibling generation. While the emphasis of this book is on cousins, we believe the more that siblings set the stage for their sons and daughters, the better. If you are a sibling owner, this book should help you create the circumstances to help your children become a successful team—if it's the family's goal to continue in business together.

This book anticipates that the cousin generation will contain five to fifteen or more members. But suppose you have only a small number of cousins in the cousin generation. Perhaps the founding parents had two children who in turn each had two children and now there are four cousins in the third generation. You will learn what to do if your family has only a limited number in the cousin generation.

We have written extensively about sibling partnerships and, in fact, an earlier book in the Family Business Leadership Series is devoted to them (*Making Sibling Teams Work: The Next Generation*). *From Siblings to Cousins* now turns its attention to what we like to refer to as the "Cousin Collaboration," an extension of the siblings' active cooperation that is necessary to a thriving family firm. You will learn more about what we mean by a Cousin Collaboration and how it functions in later chapters.

It is our hope that this book will serve as a valuable resource to family members in cousin-owned businesses or businesses that are about to be cousin owned. Our intent is that the ideas presented here and the questions we raise all become topics for discussion at cousin meetings and other family forums. That will enable the family as a whole to increase its understanding of the requirements for success in the cousin stage and subsequent generations.

By our estimates, about 16 percent of family businesses are cousin owned. But there is more knowledge available than ever before about how to make a successful transition to the cousin generation and how cousins themselves can work together effectively. We've packed as much of that knowledge into this book as we can. We believe that the more business-owning families know, the more they can dispel the old cliché that family firms wither away in the third generation.

. . . about 16 percent of family businesses are cousin owned.

Chapter 2

A World of Difference

Cousins and the world in which they grow up are vastly different from siblings and the world that shaped them. These changing conditions have a profound impact on family dynamics and on how cousins can most effectively own and run a business together.

Consider a family we'll call the Harrisons, owners of Harrison Automotive, a very successful Midwest supplier to the auto industry. All in their late 50s and early 60s, the four Harrison siblings—Angela, Sarah, Thom, and Andy—remember vividly how their father, the founder of the family business, ruled it with an iron fist.

"He expected us to do what he told us, and no disagreeing with him was allowed," recalled Angela.

"Even after we'd worked in the company 20 years," said Thom.

"Remember how furious he was when we told him that we just couldn't operate the business the way he did?" added Sarah. "He just didn't understand that we couldn't copy his management style and still function as a team."

"Thank goodness Mom was there to smooth things over all the time," Andy mused. "If it hadn't been for her, I'd have left the business."

. . . one generation can't run the business the same way the previous generation did.

"Me, too," said Sarah. "But our experiences with Dad did teach us that one generation can't run the business the same way the previous generation did. You can't even run the family the same way."

The Harrison siblings inherited equal shares of the family business. All still work in it—Andy is chief executive officer, Thom is corporate counsel, Sarah heads advertising and marketing, and Angela, about to retire, is vice president of human resources. They have worked well as a team over the years and, as a result, the company has grown and prospered. It now has 4500 employees.

Among them, the siblings have 14 children ranging in age from late teens to late 30s. Three of the older cousins have worked in the business a decade or more and have risen to responsible positions—president/chief operating officer, chief financial officer, and vice president of information systems. The two youngest cousins are still in college and haven't decided whether they want to join the business. (They know that if they want to work in the company, they have to meet the family's requirements for employment and jobs that match their talents have to be available.)

The remaining nine cousins are pursuing careers outside the family business in other industries. Seven of the cousins live in other parts of the country. Six of them are married and so far, the Harrison siblings have 12 grandchildren.

CHANGING CONDITIONS IN THE FAMILY

The Harrison family epitomizes what we mean when we say there is a world of difference between the sibling generation and the offspring cousins. Consider the following:

♦ **Siblings have more shared experiences than cousins do.** Siblings generally grow up together in the same household and share the same set of parents. Cousins aren't subject to the kind of intimacy that brothers and sisters share. The cousins grow up in separate households and have different sets of parents.

◆ **Brothers and sisters are likely to experience that intense phenomenon known as "sibling rivalry."** Patterns of behavior developed at an early age can haunt their adult relationships. As one man in business with his older brother complained, "I'm 40 and my brother is 44, but there are times when suddenly I'm 10 again and he's 14." Nevertheless, strong feelings of kinship exist between siblings and they look out for one another.

While there's less rivalry among cousins, there is also less of a sense that "we have to take care of each other." But cousins also have the opportunity to enjoy friendships with each other that are unencumbered by the shared and often "loaded" childhood experiences of siblings.

◆ **While siblings may stay geographically close, work in the business together, and share similar values, cousins become more diverse.** Like half of the Harrison cousins, many leave home and settle in other communities. Values and points of view diverge, influenced by the spouses that the siblings brought into the family and ultimately by the cousins' own spouses. Some cousins may join the business, but most typically make different career choices. Not everyone in the cousin group feels the passionate commitment to the business that nearly everyone in the family had in the founder and sibling stages. Some cousins may not even wish to be owners of the family business.

Diversity and loosening family ties in the cousin generation pose two major challenges that we will be exploring further in the coming chapters: how to build shareholders' voluntary commitment to the family enterprise and how to hold the family together.

CHANGING CONDITIONS IN THE BUSINESS

The changes that take place in the family as it moves from siblings to cousins result in changes in the family's business as well. Here are some key examples:

◆ In the sibling stage, most or all of the family members work in the business. But in the cousin generation, proportionately fewer family members are likely to be employed in the business. Many of the cousins may not have the skills needed by the business or may simply wish to pursue careers in other fields.

◆ Family members usually hold the top family business leadership positions in the sibling generation. In the cousin stage, there's a higher probability that non-family executives will rise to CEO, chairman, or other key posts.

◆ In the sibling generation, all or nearly all the family members serve on the board of directors. In the cousin generation, however, there are more family members than director slots, and in many instances, the family has moved to strengthen the board by adding talented, independent directors.

> . . . forcing equality on cousins can lead to the
> very conflict that equality was suppose to avoid.

◆ The family enterprise most likely began as one business. By the time the cousins arrive on the scene, it may well have evolved into a complicated portfolio of subsidiaries and independent businesses with interlocking ownership—different corporations or partnerships owned by various configurations of the family.

◆ Equal treatment of family members is often a key to success in the sibling stage. Siblings may inherit equal shares of the business, have equal pay, and have an equal voice in decisions. By the cousin stage, treating everyone the same is typically no longer realistic or viable. Compensation is more likely to be based on market rates and merit. Additionally, some cousins may inherit larger ownership positions than others. While equality may help siblings to avoid conflict, forcing equality on cousins who bring different skills and talents to the family business can lead to the very conflict that equality was suppose to avoid.

EXHIBIT 1   How Conditions Change

Siblings	Cousins
In the family:	*In the family:*
Have the same parents and grow up in the same household.	Have different parents and grow up in different homes.
Share common life experiences.	Have varied life experiences.
Experience sibling rivalry.	Have less rivalry.
Look out for one another.	Feel less responsibility toward one another.
Live close to one another as adults.	Are more diverse geographically.
In the business:	*In the business:*
More family members are employed in the business than not.	A smaller percentage of family members are employed in the business.
Family members hold most of the top leadership positions.	More non-family executives rise to the key posts.
The number of family board members is about equal to the number of family members.	The board has more independent directors and fewer family members.

Continued

EXHIBIT 1 **Continued**

Siblings	Cousins
Siblings may receive equal pay and be treated equally in other ways.	Cousins' compensation is based on market rates and merit; equal treatment is no longer viable.
The family is engaged in one enterprise.	The family is engaged in multiple enterprises.
Shareholders are likely to be equally distributed among siblings.	Cousins may inherit considerably different sized ownership stakes in the family business.

MOVING TO A "COUSIN COLLABORATION"

All of the differences described above have implications for how the family is organized and for how the business is managed in the third stage. A Sibling Partnership was the center of the family organization and of business leadership and ownership in the sibling generation. Now that the family and the business are both larger and more complicated, the family must move toward a different form of teamwork and leadership. We call it the "Cousin Collaboration."

We like the word "collaboration" because it has such a positive connotation. The very definition of "collaborate" is "to work together." **The key to a Cousin Collaboration is that it is voluntary. Each of the individuals involved is making a conscious commitment to work together with the others toward certain agreed-upon goals.**

In a true Cousin Collaboration, the cousins come together because it's something they want to do. They aren't coerced by their parents to do it, and while they may be influenced by their history and the legacy that the business represents, they don't feel bound by their history and that legacy. They also know they have the freedom to opt out. By this time, the family has probably given deliberate attention to liquidity issues and drawn up guidelines whereby family members can sell shares.

A goal of the Cousin Collaboration is to make remaining an owner so satisfying that opting out is rare. Maintaining the commitment of shareholders is important because doing so helps to hold the family together and to retain financial and leadership resources for the business. It represents the next generation of the healthy family/healthy business paradigm necessary for family business success.

The chapters that follow illustrate how Cousin Collaborations work in the business and in the family and provide guidelines on what it takes to continue a family business into the third generation and beyond.

SIBLINGS CAN SET THE STAGE

The members of the sibling generation play a very powerful role in setting the stage for family and business success in the cousin generation. Most important is raising and educating children who are capable of meaningfully and thoughtfully considering all the issues that face a business-owning family.

When the siblings themselves work together effectively, they serve as a model for the next generation. They create the mechanisms that not only serve themselves well but that will also enable their children, the cousins, to function effectively as a group. This typically means that an active board is in place, including competent, outside directors. It means that the family is bound by a process of family meetings and decision making, usually based on a family mission statement. It means that the siblings have created functioning structures, processes, and policies that will enable their adult children to move forward together and make the decisions appropriate to their own generation. If the siblings have not accomplished these tasks, the sibling generation's work has not been completed, leaving their children the challenge and danger of tasks unfinished.

> When the siblings themselves work together effectively, they serve as a model for the next generation . . . [T]he rules change when the cousins take over from the siblings.

Like the Harrison siblings described at the beginning of this chapter, the siblings understand that just as they could not operate the way their parents did, a Cousin Collaboration cannot function the same way a Sibling Partnership does. The cousins must carry on in a manner that meets the present and future needs of the family and the business, not the needs of the past. Just as all the rules changed when the family business went from the founding generation to the siblings, so must the rules change when the cousins take over from the siblings.

Siblings who want to know more about Sibling Partnerships and how they can prepare a family and a business for the next generation will find it useful to refer to *Making Sibling Teams Work: The Next Generation.*

HOW COUSINS CAN PREPARE THEMSELVES

Of course, it's not just the siblings who have to do the work of preparing for the cousins to take over. Cousins have to prepare themselves as well.

There are two major ways in which cousins can do this:

1. Cousins should educate themselves to be effective owners of the company. There's a book on that topic, too, in the Family Business Leadership Series, *Family Business Ownership: How to Be an Effective Shareholder.* It will provide you with basic information about what it means to be a family business owner and what you need to know. Essentially, you will want to read all you can about business basics and how they pertain to the business you own.

You will want to read everything the company distributes to its shareholders as well, so that you understand the company and the direction it's going.

Cousins show wisdom when they realize that the shares they hold in the family business are a major asset and need to be attended to responsibly.

If you are not working in the company, ideally you will be what we call an "active owner." An active owner takes a genuine interest in the family business and is concerned with all its issues. Hopefully you will not be a "passive owner" (simply collecting your dividends and making no conscious decision about staying an owner) or an "investor owner" (like a passive owner but makes a conscious decision to continue as an owner as long as returns are satisfactory).

Cousins show wisdom when they realize that the shares they hold in the family business are a major asset and need to be attended to responsibly.

2. Develop constructive relationships with one another. Get to know each other. Get together as a group and talk about your hopes for the family business under your watch and consider the kinds of issues that may arise and confront you as a group. You'll need to begin discussing questions such as: How do we organize the family? How will people have appropriate opportunities for input? How do we make decisions in a larger group? How do we secure commitment as shareholders?

By this generation, cousins may not know one another very well, even though they now own a business together. Geography may separate them. Some cousins find that when they finally get together, they have a great time and that it's more about family than it is about the business. Often, someone in the cousin generation has to take the initiative to make getting together happen.

You might start with a reunion or a family retreat. Don't be surprised if you enjoy one other much more than you expected. That's a benefit that will stand both the family and the business in good stead.

Actually, there's a third thing you as a cousin can do to prepare for transfer of the business to your generation. If you aspire to work in the business, be sure you are well educated and experienced so you can make a genuine contribution. Not everyone in the cousin generation can work and advance in the business. You have to earn the right to do so.

WHAT A HEALTHY FAMILY BUSINESS LOOKS LIKE

What does a healthy family business look like as the sibling stage draws to a close and what does it look like once the transition to the cousins is complete?

On the eve of making a transition to the cousin stage, while the business is still in the hands of the siblings, the siblings are already behaving a lot like it's a cousin business. As suggested earlier, they will have anticipated and begun to develop and execute the mechanisms and processes that will be needed in the cousin stage: strategic planning, business and family governance systems, family business policies, and so on.

The siblings will also be turning to the cousin generation for guidance and input on how to design the business for future generations. In other words, the siblings are encouraging the cousins to participate in the design because the cousins are the ones who will have to live with it.

> . . . a healthy family business is dynamic and interactive.

The siblings will have managed to avoid poisonous fiefdoms, in which each has sole control of a unit or subsidiary because they have never learned to get along with one another. They have prepared their children to get along with their siblings and cousins. And, they have prepared the children to take an interest in the business and to educate themselves about it.

Ideally, the siblings will be handing over a business that is profitable and strategically sound. The family will be proud of this legacy and will be committed to its continued success.

Once the cousin generation is firmly entrenched, a healthy family business is dynamic and interactive. Family members trust one another and have the confidence and ability to adapt their structures and processes, as necessary, over time. They constantly examine how they do things and talk about how to improve what they do.

Once the cousin generation is firmly entrenched, a healthy family business is dynamic and interactive.

There is a sense of unity, seeing themselves as one family and one enterprise. They increasingly move away from thinking of this family branch or that, an attitude that can lead to rancor and divisiveness. And, however many businesses the family may own, they are seen as part of the whole.

The cousins also effectively manage what can be the pendulum-like swings between putting business first and putting family first. They accomplish more stability in balancing the needs of family with the needs of the business because the business may be larger and more thoroughly established than in earlier generations. At the same time, family policies may exist to govern family expectations about employment, compensation, distributions, perks, and other matters that may have allowed family considerations to have been asserted in the business. An understanding has been developed that if "family first" practices go too far, the business will be compromised. If taking care of the business and protecting it, however, means ignoring the family, then alienated family owners can sap the family business system's strength. As a result, the cousins become very adaptable in balancing family and business.

By the cousin stage, the demands of a larger and much more complicated business often mean that the family itself cannot produce sufficient leadership for management and oversight. It must rely on greater involvement of non-family executives to manage the company and must include sophisticated, experienced outsiders on the board to provide insight and independent oversight. And while the ties between the family and management, between the family and the board, and among the family members themselves are loosened, the family and the business can still be each other's greatest assets.

Chapter 3

Re-energizing the Family

When we consult with a group of cousins in a business-owning family, we nearly always open the proceedings with two questions: **"Do you want to continue to own this business together? If so, why?"** These are the most critical questions the cousins have to answer and we urge them to be particularly thoughtful as they explore the questions together. It's important that they not make the assumption that everyone wants to continue together. Continuing to be an owner should be a conscious, voluntary choice. That's what "collaboration" implies, after all.

Continuing to be an owner should be a conscious, voluntary choice.

Typically, an ancillary question is: "Do *all* of us want to continue to own this business, or are there individuals in the group who would rather not continue as owners?" If there are some who prefer to change their status, they should have the opportunity at some point to opt out. Forcing them to remain owners by not providing liquidity opportunities invites serious difficulties. They should not be inevitably bound financially to the organization. The core group of cousins who wish to continue to be owners can then move forward together.

TWO MAJOR REASONS

When cousins answer yes to the first question, they generally cite variations on one of two major reasons:

1. "The business represents an important set of values to us and gives us an opportunity to continue and/or strengthen a legacy that is larger than ourselves."
2. "We're better off being part of an aggregated pool of capital and we'll have better management of and better returns on that capital as part of a group of relatives than if we try to manage our assets alone."

We've known some cousin groups that have such an overwhelming and passionate commitment to the family business that they would never contemplate selling it. The heritage that the business represents completely overshadows any monetary considerations.

For cousins who don't work in the business, staying an owner in many ways may be an economically irrational decision. Liquidity is limited (shares can't be sold by a simple call to a stockbroker). A high percentage of their personal wealth may be tied up in the business. With little diversification, they may be exposed to greater financial risk. They may be rich on paper, but not in pocket.

So why would anybody want to own 5 percent or 10 percent (or less) of a company that they don't work in, that's far from where they live, and that probably doesn't give them much reward in terms of dividends? Sometimes there may be little choice if no readily available method exists to sell. But sometimes they *choose* to own for emotional reasons. They might feel a sense of identification with the family through their ownership of the business. They might revere the family values that are exemplified in the business and wish to pass those values on to their children. Being an owner might provide networking opportunities that enhance a cousin's career. Or cousins might believe in the social purpose of the company.

Still, some cousins may feel that the financial advantages are the most attractive factor in deciding to continue together as owners. One may say, "I'm the heir to considerable wealth, but I've never developed the skills to manage it or even to manage people who do. If I stay an owner, my investment will be managed for me and I'll get a good return on my inheritance." An ideal justification for staying an owner? Probably not. But it's realistic. We often see cousins continue ownership because of hoped-for monetary gain.

The reasons for owning a business together could be visualized as a continuum, with the cherished legacy at one end and the financial considerations at the other. Often, however, the cousins who cite "values" as the reason for continuing ownership together include economic value as one dimension. While they may emphasize social purpose or religious belief as critical, they also embrace the desirability of a good financial return.

The reasons for owning a business together could be visualized as a continuum, with the cherished legacy at one end and the financial considerations at the other.

As a cousin group deliberates if and why it wants to continue as owners together, it also should consider strategic dimensions that are involved. The group should discuss its willingness to continue to make the investments required for the business to remain competitive and how it might respond if an opportunity arises to sell the business to a competitor. If the company is in a consolidating industry, should this business seek acquisitions or look for potential buyers? If some cousins do not wish to continue to be owners, how will providing them with liquidity affect the company?

Other issues that cousins must address concern leadership. Should top leadership positions go only to family members? If so, will the family have enough sufficiently qualified and experienced members to fill those positions?

What's important now is to be able to consciously say, "We're willing to do what's necessary in terms of investment, in terms of disciplining ourselves, and in terms of our expectations about how this business is governed and operated, to be a viable entity going forward. We're also aware that we will probably have to change our strategy to move forward successfully."

AN EXCITING OPPORTUNITY

Let's assume that you and your cousins have gone through the discussions described above and have committed yourselves to continuing as owners together. A significant reason for doing so is that you are proud of what the business contributes to the community, but you also know it can provide you and your family with a nice financial reward. You want to give your children a chance to participate in their legacy. Some of the cousins work in the business, others don't. Some live in the town where the business is located, others live in other communities and even other states. All have the different perspectives and different interests that are typical of cousins. How can such a diverse group assure profitability, fulfillment of social objectives, and achievement of the goal of passing it on to the next generation?

To continue together effectively, cousins should attend to creating, strengthening, or re-energizing a family organization. The first step in this process is to take advantage of the huge opportunity to rethink what the family has done in the past and begin to make conscious decisions about how your generation wants to go forward together. You can apply this opportunity to virtually everything you can think of.

. . . it is a sense of shared values that holds a family organization together.

The place to start is with the family's values. We put this first because, in our experience, it is a sense of shared values that holds a family organization together. Because cousins are more diverse than their parents were, it is all the more necessary for them to discuss values to determine commonalities and differences. As a group, cousins can consider the family's values statement, if there is one, and give it a thorough review. The discussion can explore such questions as:

- What has fairness meant in our family in the past and what is it going to mean in the future?
- What has equality meant in our family in the past and what is it going to mean in the future?
- What has responsibility meant in our family in the past and what is it going to mean in the future?
- What has accountability meant in our family in the past and what is it going to mean in the future?

If your family does not yet have a values statement, we encourage you and your cousins to go to work on developing one. **The point of looking at values first is to understand your core—those fundamental commitments on which your family has built its business and which family members make to one another.** As much as possible, the next generation should sustain that for which the family has always stood, bearing in mind that some things may need reinterpretation or modification to fit current circumstances.

Suppose the Harrison family that you met in the last chapter began work on a family values statement. It might look something like this:

EXHIBIT 2   **Harrison Family Values Statement**

We believe in:

- Following the Golden Rule: treat others as you wish to be treated.
- Family unity and caring for one another.
- Honesty and integrity in all that we do.
- Contributing to the community and leaving the world a better place than we found it.
- Celebrating and enjoying the gift of life.
- The power of education.
- The human rights and equality of all people.
- Respecting diversity within and outside our family.
- The importance of hard work and discipline.

"To simplify our customers' lives" is the core purpose identified by Wawa, Inc., a family-owned chain of more than 540 convenience stores, headquartered in Wawa, Pennsylvania. In addition, Wawa proudly touts its core values: value people, delight customers, embrace change, do the right thing, do things right, and have a passion for winning.

"These values have driven the company's growth," says Richard D. Wood Jr., Wawa's fifth-generation chairman and retired CEO. "If these values were not practiced, there would be a lack of alignment around strategies."[1]

Another Pennsylvania family that understands the importance of its values is the Hatfield, Pennsylvania–based Clemens family, which owns Hatfield Quality Meats with about half a billion dollars in sales and over 40 related owners. The Clemens clan is dedicated to treating employees well and to giving back to the community. Focusing on these treasured values enabled the family to agree to some exceptionally difficult decisions that were necessary to restore the company to financial health.

One of those decisions involved removing two high-level family employees.[2]

Additional information on values can be found in *Family Business Values: How to Assure a Legacy of Continuity and Success.*

Once the cousins have reconsidered and, if necessary, reformulated a statement of the family's values, they can turn their attention to such precedents as family traditions, policy statements, and the structure of the family organization itself. The weight of prior decisions or non-decisions accumulates over time and over generations. As a group, the cousins can explore what their grandparents and parents did or failed to do that might stand in the way of long-term family business success.

In a spirit of renewal and recommitment, the cousins can question everything, respecting the past but making the changes necessary to adapt the family and the business to present and future circumstances.

STRUCTURING THE FAMILY ORGANIZATION

Family businesses excel when they have good management and a well-functioning board of directors. But research also shows that a self-perpetuating and self-regulating family organization contributes to the longevity of family businesses.[3]

By "family organization," we mean whatever structures and procedures are used to hold a family together and sustain its commitment to the business. As the family becomes larger and more far-flung, and as the business depends on more non-family executives and relatively fewer family members for leadership, family organization becomes more important to creating and maintaining the cohesion necessary to support the business and give family members a sense of family and of belonging.

... a self-perpetuating and self-regulating family organization contributes to the longevity of family businesses.

A family organization serves many important purposes. It:

- Enables cousins and other family members to get to know one another and to build relationships among themselves.
- Promotes understanding of the family business and the family legacy.
- Trains family members to be effective shareholders.
- Makes decisions about how to shape the family for the future.
- Makes sure that family members are prepared to lead the business, if that is the family's choice.
- Provides valuable roles for family members to play even though they are not working in the business.
- Oversees the preparation of family members to fill leadership positions in the family.

In short, a family organization is what keeps "family" in the family business.

In a smaller family, a family organization can be as simple as having an executive committee of family members or a family council. In larger families, it can mean having a family council with numerous committees, holding family retreats or reunions and regular family meetings, and establishing a family foundation or a family office overseen by a board of family members.

. . . a family organization is what keeps "family" in the family business.

Simply put, **"family organization" means that, in some way, the family has organized itself and adopted some form of governance.** Perhaps nothing energizes a family more than an effective family organization, because it makes the family conscious of itself as a family and encourages members to think beyond personal interests and to act for the good of other family members and the family as a whole.

In many ways, a family organization fulfills the role that "Mom" probably filled in the first generation of the family business—making sure the family's needs were met and that the business and the family supported each other. Family leadership in the cousin generation, however, is more difficult than simply picking up where Grandmother left off, because the family is larger and more complex. Thought should be given to how to encourage and nurture family members to take up the family leadership challenge and how to reward them when they do—not by paying them, necessarily, but by showing them adequate appreciation.

ANOTHER CRITICAL QUESTION

Early in this chapter, we cited some questions that were critical for cousins to answer. Now, as the cousins are ready to structure the family organization, there is another critical question: "Are we all one family or many families?"

One of the chief roadblocks to family business success in the cousin generation is branch conflict, which occurs when the children of each sibling see their family line—instead of the extended family—as their family. Rivalries that existed among the sibling generation now get played out in the cousin generation as each branch acts in its own self-interest and competes with the others.

"Are we all one family or many families?"

In some of the smartest cousin-generation businesses that we know, the cousins have consciously come together and decided that "we are one family." They put behind them the rivalries and animosities that afflicted their parents in the sibling generation, often finding that they can make friends with their cousins. They commit themselves to the good of the business and the extended family, not just their line of the family.

The best-known example of this kind of decision making is offered by Susan E. Tifft and Alex S. Jones in their book *The Trust: The Private and Powerful Family Behind The New York Times.* They point out that in 1995, the 13 cousins of the Sulzberger family, owners of the New York Times Company, declared their wish to regard themselves as members of one family and not as members of four branches. Out of that desire, Tifft and Jones write, came the decision to combine the sibling generation's four separate trusts, which held 85 percent of the public company's controlling Class B stock, into a single trust "in which every member of the cousins' generation and their children stood to share equally."[4]

That decision meant a great financial sacrifice on the part of two of the cousins, who accepted one-thirteenth stakes rather than the one-eighth they would have inherited if trusts were not combined. For them, the mission of the newspaper and the unity of the family were more important.

Every generation of a business-owning family needs to ask whether the members see themselves as one family or as members of a branch or as a group of individuals. Parents can help the next generation by setting up procedures and precedents that will encourage their children to be prepared to review this question for themselves, without feeling bound by the way their parents answered the question.

Some cousin groups come to the conclusion that they are not "one family." Nevertheless, they still are successful as owners and stewards of the family business because they find ways to unite behind the business without requiring every member of the group to be in lock-step with everyone else.

It's a matter of making a conscious decision and balancing individual needs with the needs of the business and the family as a whole. While the Sulzbergers chose to be one family, they nevertheless provided room for individuality. The cousins span different religions, political viewpoints, and careers, yet all are tremendously committed to the institution that is their family business. They recognize that they can all speak with the same voice while still maintaining their individuality.

STRENGTHENING THE BONDS

A strong family organization continually energizes and renews a family because there are so many vital roles to play and decisions to be made. Filling leadership positions such as family council president, committee chair, or family retreat planner keeps individuals thinking about the good of the family and how the family can support its legacy and its business. Having a voice in decisions not only strengthens the bonds among individuals in the family but also the bonds between the family and its business.

A family that renews and re-energizes itself with each succeeding generation is one that is capable of redefining and revitalizing its business. One family we know initially saw its business mission as serving God. Over the generations, that purpose was redefined as serving others. Instead of tithing to the church, the family put 10 percent of the business's profits into scholarship programs for its employees' children.

A family that renews and re-energizes itself with each succeeding generation is one that is capable of redefining and revitalizing its business.

Another family originally believed that it was more important to provide jobs in the community than for family members to receive dividends. A later generation, while it remained committed to the business's employees and its community, found that it couldn't take the company's survival for granted, as the family had done in the past. More attention had to be given to running an effective business for the long term.

It's essential that the cousins and each succeeding generation give thought to every aspect of how the family relates to its
business and make conscious decisions that reflect the needs of
the family and the business with respect to the world as it now
exists.

Chapter 4

The Requirements for Success

If a business-owning family can successfully make its last major transition, the transition to the cousin stage, then it has achieved a secure foundation for becoming a "dynasty." We use that word not to mean a succession of family rulers but to mean "everlasting." And some family businesses around the globe do seem to be lasting forever. While a number of family businesses take pride in still going strong after 200 years or more, at least two businesses in Japan have endured more than 1,000 years in the same family.

In the cousin stage, a successful business increasingly acts like a public company. Employment and compensation are based on merit, not on membership in the family. There is more strategic planning and accountability. The organization is, on the whole, much more oriented toward professionalized systems and processes.

In the cousin stage, a successful business increasingly acts like a public company.

Earlier, you learned that the cousin generation is as different from the sibling generation as the siblings were different from the founding generation. Because of these differences, the rules for running a family business and managing an effective family change with each generation. Take a quick look at Exhibit 3, "Cousin Stage Transition Issues." In the column on the left, you will see the characteristics that marked the family and its business during the reign of the siblings. In the column on the right, you will find the attributes that mark success in the cousin stage. As the business moves from the siblings to the cousins, the cousins will want adopt the attributes that will help assure their generation's success.

EXHIBIT 3   Cousin Stage Transition Issues

Siblings		Cousins
1. Fiefdoms	→	One enterprise
2. Branches	→	One family
3. Business as glue	→	Business as a means
4. Equality	→	Merit and inequality
5. Family leads business	→	Important non-family roles
6. Business leadership equals family leadership	→	Separation of family, business, and governance
7. Expected employment for family members	→	Restricted employment of family members
8. Hands-on ownership	→	"Active" ownership
9. Supportive, "advisory" board	→	Critical, "fiduciary" board
10. One form of involvement	→	Multiple forms of involvement
11. Family office within the business	→	Separate family office
12. All family on family council	→	Representative family council
13. Exclusive values	→	Inclusive values
14. Informal education	→	Active education

Siblings		Cousins
15. Expected commitment	→	Voluntary commitment
16. Unanimous (near) consensus	→	Democracy
17. Business charity	→	Family philanthropy

Let's take these 17 transition issues one by one:

1. From "fiefdoms" to "one enterprise." In an effort to avoid conflict, brothers and sisters in a family firm very often find their own special niches. One of them oversees one business and the other has another business. Or, one manages accounting, another oversees production, and another runs marketing. They stay out of each other's way, but they tend to have minimal coordination. Silos become the order of the day.

The cousins need to put an end to such fiefdoms and think of the family enterprise, however complex it may be, as one enterprise. Suppose one sibling, Jewel, runs the retail end of the business while her brother, Tyrone, oversees the customer service department. If Jewel brings her children into the retail business and Tyrone brings his into the customer service area, what they're really doing is creating neighborhoods of personal interest.

We advise cousins to abandon the idea that family members can specialize in their own domains. Instead, the cousins need to see the family firm as one enterprise and to manage it in the best interest of the totality of the business, not in a way that satisfies the personal interests of individual family members. The cousins should be able to say, "Our business is worth perpetuating as a special institution, not simply as a way of life for ourselves."

2. From "branches" to "one family." In the last chapter, we pointed out that one of the critical questions cousins have to answer is, "Are we one family or many?" While cousins can still be successful if they feel they are many families, our bias is toward regarding the cousins as one family. Again, thinking in terms of branches potentially perpetuates competition, rivalry, or conflict initiated in the sibling generation and invites each line of the family to behave primarily in its own self-interest. Each branch may feel entitled to representation on the board and protecting or advancing its own branch members, potentially at the expense of others. Distrust can build. It is better for the cousins to think of themselves as a clan or a community, not as a group of branches. An environment of community encourages cousins to act in ways that serve the interests of the entire family as well as the totality of the business.

3. From "business as glue" to "business as a means." In the sibling stage, the business often holds brothers and sisters together. In the next generation, however, the business may serve as only one of the forces holding the family together. If the business is the only glue, people tend to feel that the only way to get recognition in the family is through the business. People may begin to develop unhealthy attitudes, such as "Everybody should have a right to be on the board" or "Everybody has a right to a job in the company." Such attitudes, particularly if acted on, are obviously not good for the business or the family.

In the cousin stage, there are other means that hold family members together. In addition to the business, these reasons may include philanthropy, family organization, family reunions, retreats and vacations, other family investments, shared family activities, or special family communications (newsletters, websites, group e-mails, etc.). The family organization that we talked about in Chapter 4 can play a huge role in making sure that the business is not the only means of keeping the family close.

4. From "equality" to "merit and inequality." If we're members of the sibling stage, we very likely treat each other equally. With equal ownership positions, equal incomes—we have equal almost everything. In the cousin stage, that's impossible.

Cousins inevitably have unequal economic situations and unequal life chances. If there were two siblings and one had two children and the other had three, the three children of the second sibling will individually inherit less than each of the two children of the first. Out of necessity, a cousin business adopts a merit system of hiring, compensation, and promotions, so only those who have a real contribution to make to the enterprise get hired, and pay and advancement for family members are no longer equal. Outcomes may also be unequal. For example, as your cousin, I may have inherited more than you, but my child might become a social worker while yours becomes a successful entrepreneur who is wealthier than anybody else in the family.

Basically, cousins have to get comfortable with inequality. It has to be accepted. They just can't be equal in everything— not in economics, not in their lifestyles, and not even in their ability to contribute to the business.

The cousins need to be mindful that the business needs to hire the best possible key executives, whether or not they are family.

---

5. From "family leads business" to "important non-family roles." Nearly all the key positions in a family company are held by family members in the sibling stage. In the cousin stage, however, the business will have some non-family people who are playing critical roles, perhaps even as president or CEO. Non-family senior managers may outnumber family senior managers. The cousins need to be mindful that the business needs to hire the best possible key executives, whether or not they are family.

6. From "business leadership equals family leadership" to "separation of family, business, and governance." During the founding and the sibling stages, those people who lead the business usually tend to be the same people who lead the family and the business's board of directors. Cousins, however, often separate these roles. Some will lead the business, others will lead the board, and still others will lead the family.

More often than not, a family council becomes necessary in the cousin stage. Sometimes councils are started in the form of family meetings during the sibling stage, but they become more formal organizations when the cousins take charge.

7. From "expected employment for family members" to "restricted employment of family members." Generally, in the sibling stage, a high percentage of the family may join the business. When a family business reaches the cousin stage, however, wise families make their policies more and more restrictive with regard to the employment of family members. Employment is based more and more on merit and on increasingly higher standards of merit. The goal is no longer to attract every family member into the business. Instead, it now must aim at attracting those who are most qualified.

8. From "hands-on ownership" to "'active' ownership." In the early stages of a family business, owners are "hands-on"—with the responsibility for running the business. In the cousin stage, however, ownership is more dispersed and a smaller percentage of owners actually work in the business. The rest of the shareholders may not visit the business site very often but, as we have suggested in Chapter 2, they can and should function as "active" or "involved" owners. As we stated in our book on effective ownership, active owners "are attentive to the issues facing a family business. They develop relationships with top management, they make it a point to understand the company strategy, and they take the time to promote the culture of the business. In other words, they take a genuine interest in the company, offer support to management, and involve themselves as appropriate."[5]

... active owners "are attentive to the issues facing a family business."

---

9. From "supportive, 'advisory' board" to "critical, 'fiduciary' board." The company's board of directors during the sibling stage tends to be advisory and supportive in nature. Board members may say, "You've heard our opinions. It's your company. Do what you think is best."

In the cousin stage, however, many owners won't have a seat at the board table. The cousins, therefore, need a board that takes more responsibility for the destiny of the company. They need board members who will say, "Our first job is to assure account-ability because we represent the collective goals and values of *all* shareholders." In a cousin-owned business, the board becomes a much more formalized body representing the interests of all of ownership.

10. From "one form of involvement" to "multiple forms of involvement." During the sibling stage, the primary way to be involved in the family business is to work in it. Cousins can take advantage of many opportunities to make a contribution to the business in ways other than working in it. They can serve on the board or on the family council. They can be good, active own-ers. They can plan social events that enhance family cohesion. They can help direct the family's philanthropic activities.

11. From "family office within the business" to "separate fam-ily office." The purpose of a family office is to take care of the family's personal interests—such as income tax preparation, making sure there's adequate life insurance, determining how to invest the family's money, or making arrangements for the fami-ly's vacation home. In the sibling stage, such matters are usually handled inside the company with the aid of personal assistants or the company's finance, accounting, legal, or other staff.

It becomes more appropriate in the cousin stage to move the family office function out of the company and into a separate organization. That way, the family can be clear about who is getting what services at whose expense and can be sure that the business is not paying for services that should be paid for by the family.

12. From "all family on family council" to "representative family council." In the sibling era, family meetings are held and everyone shows up to discuss and makes decisions about matters concerning the family. In essence, the family members function as a committee of the whole. They may or may not call themselves a "family council."

When the family gets larger—15, 18, or 50 or more members—a committee of the whole becomes unworkable. Cousin Collaborations find it more practical to turn to a subgroup of the family to serve as a family council representing the extended family.

13. From "exclusive values" to "inclusive values." Rules of conduct tend to be more specific, more defined, and more strictly enforced in the sibling stage. Violations can become major issues and major sources of conflict. Cousins need more flexibility, tolerance, and more acceptance of deviation from norms. They are best served by learning to look at the glass as half full rather than half empty.

Successful cousin/owners find reasons to accept and relate to one another, not reasons to disagree and debate. Instead of fretting over differences, they focus on common values. They accept that individuals will identify and stay connected to the family and the business for different reasons. They seek out the shared views and interests that work to hold family members together rather than instituting a set of norms that all are expected to follow.

14. From "informal education" to "active education." Business-owning families often set up special learning experiences for family members. Whatever family education takes place in the sibling generation, however, tends to be informal and ad hoc. If a family meeting is scheduled, one of the siblings may invite an expert in to talk about communications or estate planning.

Successful Cousin Collaborations actively plan for family education. They may have a formal curriculum. The family council might appoint an education committee or the council as a whole might develop an educational program. The cousins are cognizant that there are more people in the family who need education, and that certain age groups in particular—say, 15- to 20-year-olds—need introductions to several important subjects.

While some of the programs aim to educate family members about the business, others target improvement of personal skills, such as teamwork, conflict management, and effective listening. We've known some families who have conducted programs on parenting children of wealth. Sometimes education can be just plain fun—such as a walking tour in another country.

15. From "expected commitment" to "voluntary commitment." The expectation of commitment to the business in the sibling stage is so great that if a family member wants out, he may be seen as being unfaithful and disrespectful to his parents, who founded the business. He may become a *persona non grata* and experience great guilt.

Such expectations can impose a tremendous burden, however, and are not appropriate to the Cousin Collaboration. As a reader of this book, you already know that, in our view, commitment to the business in the cousin stage should be voluntary. Family members who offer that commitment should be able to do so for reasons they see as positive. Family members who wish to opt out of ownership or employment should be able to do so without fear of losing the love and respect of their relatives. Most likely, the Cousin Collaboration will function more effectively when individuals whose interests and hearts lie elsewhere are not made into emotional or financial captives.

16. From "unanimous (near) consensus" to "democracy." When two or three siblings are running a business, they have to "agree to agree" for things to function well. If it's a larger group of siblings—say, four to six—then one of them might say, "You've heard my views. I don't agree, but I'll go along with you." Consensus or near consensus is essential.

Cousins, however, can vote. "It's 14 in favor and 3 against. The ayes have it." The cousins know that's life and say, "Let's

move on." Decisions in the cousin stage can be made democrat-
ically in a number of venues—the family council, the family as a
whole, the shareholders group (by voting shares), and the board
of directors. Management of the business, however, is not such a
democratic process.

17. From "business charity" to "family philanthropy." When the
siblings are in charge, giving tends to work this way: The local
Girls Scouts troop, the cancer society, and the firefighters asso-
ciation request help. The siblings get together and decide what
they will support, and the company sends a check.

In the cousin stage, family giving is moved out of the company and into the family itself. Family members meet and decide
what to support as a family. In the best-case scenario, the family
will move from being charitable (giving to help specific causes or
organizations) to being more philanthropic (giving strategically
on a larger scale to bring about significant results). The family
may organize itself around a major theme for its giving—such as
assistance to disadvantaged children, cancer research, support of
religious or educational organizations, the eradication of AIDS,
or the advancement of the performing arts.

**The business itself will still make charitable contributions,
but it will give for business reasons, not for family reasons.** It
will do what it should to maintain its reputation as a good citi-
zen—meaning, it may still support the local Girl Scouts troop
and the firefighters. (You will find more on the topic of philanthropy in Chapter 7.)

ADDITIONAL REQUISITES

Making the transitions described above puts the cousins on the
road to success, but the journey is not yet complete. The next
exhibit, "Cousin Collaboration Essentials," lists seven additional
requirements for success. These essentials build on or complement the 17 transitions that the cousins must make.

EXHIBIT 4   Cousin Collaboration Stage Essentials

- ◆ Agreeing to disagree
- ◆ Flexible portfolio
- ◆ Buy–sells approach value
- ◆ Coordinated estate planning
- ◆ Dividend expectations are established
- ◆ Attract qualified, visible family leadership
- ◆ Patient, tolerant "pruning"

Again, let's take these points one by one:

1. Agreeing to disagree. As you saw in transition 16, the sibling generation "agrees to agree," aiming for consensus. But the cousins need to function more as a democracy, meaning that they have to figure out a way to "agree to disagree." They will need to devise ways to hear and cope with dissent. Family members will need to feel that they have a right to express their opinions even though their views may go against what others think. The cousins will need to create forums, such as family meetings and a family council, where dissent as well as agreement can be aired. They also should develop checks and balances to protect minority interests.

Focusing on their potential for joint achievement enables the cousins' business vision to be forward rather than backward looking.

---

2. Flexible portfolio. Businesses come and businesses go, and it's necessary for the cousins to be comfortable with that concept. A family can be in business forever but over time the business may change. Change is inevitable and businesses must adapt to survive.

Basically, cousins become tied to one another more because of common values and identity and what they can accomplish together than because of the memory of the business that Granddad founded. Focusing on their potential for joint achievement enables the cousins' business vision to be forward rather than backward looking.

3. Buy–sells approach value. When family members buy and sell their shares in the cousin stage, they're buying and selling at prices that more and more approximate the market value of those shares. This is in keeping with the fact that family firms in the cousin stage and beyond tend to act "as if public" and requires accountability for financial performance and careful liquidity planning. (See *Financing Transitions.*)

4. Coordinated estate planning. Estate planning needs to be coordinated so that the best advice is dispersed throughout the family and so the company isn't faced with unpleasant surprises as a result of bad estate planning. When a shareholder is faced with a large bill from the Internal Revenue Service associated with the value of inherited stock, this effort to find the cash needed to meet the obligation can involve the business, sometimes with negative impacts on strategy or performance. Coordinated estate planning helps to avoid nasty surprises.

5. Dividend expectations are established. Often family businesses set dividends at fixed amounts—or according to set formulas or policies. Family members come to expect a certain amount and sometimes depend on it. As larger, cousin-owned businesses act more "as if public," dividends are often based on some kind of formula—such as 20 percent of profits or 2 percent of the company's value. Family members should be educated about the formula so that they have realistic expectations and they understand that dividends are tied to the company's profits.

It is best if the sibling generation sets the stage for establishing dividend expectations. If they don't, the cousins should thoughtfully initiate a dividend policy based on considerations of the business's need to fund its strategy, reasonable expectations of managerial performance, and shareholder goals. Dividend policy emerges from dialogue involving top management, the board, and the family council.

6. Attract qualified, visible family leadership. Sometimes the family gets too far removed from the business at the cousin stage. With few family members in management, the family isn't as visible in the company as it might and should be. They become like absentee landlords caring primarily about the money they can take.

In the cousins generation, the family should promote the attractiveness of the business to the younger generation and enable the older cousins to find ways to contribute to the business from a cultural point of view—participating in anniversary celebrations of the business, for example, or representing the business at community events.

The cousins must find a way to strike a balance. On the financial and the professional side of the business, they want the company to be "as if public," performing competently and profitably. On the emotional and cultural side of a family business, however, it is important to maintain the family connection. Achieving that balance can make it possible for such family businesses to enjoy the best of both worlds.

7. Patient, tolerant "pruning." This refers to the willingness to let family members sell out if they no longer wish to be owners. In essence, the ability to cash in shares permits a "pruning" of reluctant owners that strengthens the remaining ownership base. "Patient" refers to taking the time to develop liquidity programs that allow those who wish to sell to do so over time with minimal injury to the business. "Tolerant" means that those who sell their shares are not condemned for doing so. Owning shares should not be a ticket required for participation in the family council, family philanthropy, family reunions, or other family activities.

... the ability to cash in shares permits a "pruning" of reluctant owners that strengthens the remaining ownership base.

Chapter 5

Special Challenges for Cousin-Owned Businesses

A family business that reaches the cousin stage has already defied the odds. It has survived many obstacles and passed many tests. Startup business fragility and the deeply emotional succession from founder to offspring are long past. The business has weathered market life cycles and developed new, successful products and processes. The family has learned to implement and to trust professional management practices and to manage and retain non-family executives.

Second-generation siblings have overcome the divisive temptations of jealousy and rivalry. No doubt the family has coped with business crises and family tragedies. Good personal financial planning has prepared the family for estate taxes and other monetary hurdles.

New issues arise as the cousins take over ownership of the business. The challenges remain great. As we have seen, cousins do not typically experience the tight bonds of siblings. Personal interests and goals become increasingly disparate as the family continues to grow. Proportionately fewer family members are involved in management, and the skills and responsibilities of those in the business can vary greatly. Some family members may have personal needs or desires for more spending power and look for dividends to provide funding. Values of family members begin to diverge and the cohesive personal charisma and loving power of early family leaders is no longer present.

Against this backdrop, here is an overview of the seven special challenges facing the cousins/owners.

1. How can we attract competent family members to employment in the business? A hallmark of family businesses is family involvement in business leadership. In the cousin stage a number of factors make it harder to draw family members to the business. The cousins are more remote from the business than their predecessors were and they don't feel compelled to join the business the way their parents did. They may look back at the previous generation and say, "Boy, there was a lot of conflict *because* the family was in the business." They clearly don't want to endure such problems.

In addition, as the business becomes larger and more complex, the family increasingly raises standards for entry into the business on the part of family members. Where once family members could join straight out of high school, now they are required to earn an advanced college degree and to get several years of work experience in another company before entering the family firm. As the bar gets set higher, family members may find the business more intimidating and less appealing.

Families in the cousin generation typically encourage offspring independence, urging the next generation to build careers on their personal choices. At the same time, such freedom to choose increases the likelihood that family members will make career commitments in places other than the family business.

One way to begin to meet this challenge is to expose family members to the business, both for fun and for personal development, when they are young. Summer jobs and internships while they are still in high school or college and opportunities to go on some business trips with others in the company help younger family members gain an appetite for the enterprise. Helping young people feel that they will be valuable to the company can stoke their interest. Young people do not necessarily understand the unique opportunities afforded by leadership in a business owned by their own family. Education is required to put both challenges and opportunities in perspective.

2. How can we introduce democracy in a fair way? Establishing democracy isn't easy. Doing so requires a process that everyone sees as fair, and family members don't always agree on what's fair. One way to approach this challenge is to establish a decision-making process before there's a real issue on the table. The goal is to design a process that everyone perceives as fair and appropriately inclusive. As cousins grapple with difficult issues, feelings may be hurt, some may take offense, others may feel left out of a decision or that communication was inadequate.

If there is a strong enough amount of goodwill and resilience in the family, you can stumble a couple of times and people will say, "Okay, now what can we learn from this and how can we improve? How do we create a better process?" (For more on "fair process," see Chapter 7.)

3. When it comes to decision making, how do we count the votes—on a per capita basis or a per share basis? Because shares are generally divided somewhat equally in the sibling generation, per capita and per share are often close to the same thing. But this becomes less true in the cousin stage and in succeeding generations.

It might seem clear that some decisions are made one way and some another. But it's not so simple. Suppose the Lopez cousins are trying to decide where to hold the next family meeting. Some of the cousins assume that the decision should be made on a one-person, one-vote basis. But another cousin jumps in and says, "But the resources that we're using to pay for all this are coming from the company, and we have different ownership interests in the company, so we ought to vote on a per share basis."

As best they can, cousins need to work toward voting one way (on a per capita basis) for family issues and another (on a per share basis) for shareholder issues. But even at shareholders' meetings, the voting issue gets complicated. Non-shareholders such as spouses and younger family members might be present. Or people may hold different amounts of shares. In such situations, shareholders might not really want to vote on a per share basis because they are unwilling to make an issue of how much ownership they have. (Legally, however, shareholder matters like electing directors or approving auditor selections have to be decided on a per share basis. If a per capita decision is made on a shareholder issue and an owner challenges it, the law should prevail.)

Cousins will find it helpful to make a separation between the family's agenda and the shareholders' agenda and to help family members understand the difference between the two. It's useful to focus on the family issues so that shareholder issues that are resolved on a per share basis don't stand out too much and make non-shareholders feel alienated. When issues must be decided on a per share basis, it may be helpful to get input from non-shareholders. Even though they can't vote, they will know they were part of the decision-making process.

Family branch issues may also emerge. One family we know considered having each family vote as a unit at family council meetings. The idea was disregarded, however, when family members realized that voting as family units could put pressure on spouses to agree with each other. They also feared that such a system would also force individuals to favor their own branch instead of the good of the whole and feared setting bad precedent for the future. Ultimately, they decided on a one-person, one-vote system on family matters.

The Cousin Collaboration involves articulating an "ownership vision."

---

4. What kind of owners do we want to be? Earlier in this book, we encouraged cousins not employed in the business to be "active owners." Such owners keep themselves informed about the issues facing the business. They develop relationships with management and offer support. And, they involve themselves in other ways as appropriate.

As a cousin, however, you could fall into some other category of ownership. You might be an "operating owner," a shareholder who also works in the business and is involved in day-to-day operations. You might be a "governing owner," sitting on the board of directors but not involved in day-to-day operations. Or, you could be a "proud owner," one who isn't really knowledgeable about the business but who is still proud to be an owner.[6]

In the sibling stage, most owners are involved in management. Cousins, however, should consider not only what kind of owners they will be individually but also as a group. The Cousin Collaboration involves articulating an "ownership vision." Should a family member always be CEO or chairman of the business? At the other extreme, a few family businesses ban family members from employment but encourage all owners to be vigilant, conscientious, and active owners. In other words, cousin owners should carefully develop a shared understanding of their relationship with their business. They should answer questions like: How should the Cousin Collaboration help shareholders conscientiously fulfill their responsibilities as owners? How will the family prepare younger family members for responsible future ownership?

5. How do we address the radical, substantial change in governance that must take place as the family business moves from a Sibling Partnership to a Cousin Collaboration? Making the transition from a smaller group of siblings to a larger group of cousins requires dramatic changes in the basic assumptions about governance. Chapter 7 describes these changes and raises the issues that the cousins must consider as the family designs and implements a new, comprehensive governance system.

6. How do we balance and manage "voice" and "exit"? This is one of the central concerns of cousin-stage businesses. In this context, "exit" means the departure of a dissatisfied owner; "voice" refers to the influence an owner can exert to rectify the cause of dissatisfaction instead of exiting. In public companies, shareholders usually express themselves by "voting with their feet"—that is, exiting by selling their stock. In family businesses the alternatives should be more nuanced than simply "love it or leave it." Please see Chapter 8 for a full discussion of this critical issue.

7. How are things different if there are only a small number of cousins? Suppose there were only two siblings in the second generation of your family business. One sibling had two children and the other, three. Now there are only five in your generation. Is yours a cousin business? Well, yes, but because the group is so small, it behaves much more like a sibling business.

What to do? Because you are more like a sibling company, lean on the sibling rules, but prepare for the cousin rules because you probably have a larger set of family members in the next generation.

These challenges tend to be unique to cousin businesses. By resolving them, the cousins not only position the family and the business for the next generation but they also create models of behavior that will support the success of the next generation of owners and leaders.

EXHIBIT 5   **Seven Special Challenges for Cousins**

1. Attracting competent family members to employment in the business
2. Introducing democracy in a fair way
3. Determining how to count the votes—on a per capita basis or per share basis?
4. Deciding what kind of owners they want to be
5. Addressing the substantial changes in governance that must take place when moving from a sibling business to a cousin business
6. Balancing and managing "voice" and "exit"
7. Dealing with the special circumstances of small cousin-owner groups

Chapter 6

Managing the Business in the Cousin Stage

As you and your cousins think about how your business should be managed while you are in charge, it is helpful to review some of the changing dynamics we described earlier. Your parents, the sibling generation, may have been seen as equals. Each probably had his or her own area of responsibility—perhaps a business within the family enterprise—and did not interfere in the others' territory. Unless an individual proved truly incompetent, they generally assumed that the sibling running a given operation was the best person to do so. The arrangement enabled the siblings to avoid many of the conflicts common in family firms.

But to be successful in the cousin generation, we have said that it is desirable to think of yourselves as one family and one enterprise. No more fiefdoms. No more promoting one's own branch of the family to the detriment of the other branches. No more assuming that the children are the best people to succeed their parents in executive or board positions.

===

... to be successful in the cousin generation, it is desirable to think of yourselves as one family and one enterprise.

===

It is likely that the family enterprise now consists of a portfolio of interlocking business segments. **Increasingly, your cousin group should be—and probably is—beginning to look more closely at how well each business is being run and to apply professionalized financial and management standards to each.**

As you proceed, your Cousin Collaboration should focus on five key areas: business strategy, leadership, employment, compensation, and managing expectations.

BUSINESS STRATEGY

It is not uncommon for businesses the age of those in the cousin stage to experience "strategic exhaustion." What that means is that the way the family has traditionally done business does not provide a viable strategy for the future. A major challenge in the cousin generation is to give thoughtful consideration to the business's strategy and make the necessary adjustments. This may call for shedding parts of the enterprise and developing others, getting into another business altogether, acquiring another business, or even selling the business or any of a number of other changes. Under the late CEO, Garry Myers III, the third generation of Columbus, Ohio–based Highlights for Children, Inc., consisting of 13 cousin-owners, expanded the company's horizons. In addition to its flagship *Highlights for Children* magazine, the business now includes eight related companies whose mission is to produce high-quality products for children and educators. Highlights is now in its fourth generation of family ownership.[7]

In many cases, a number of strategic opportunities have already been recognized and acted upon so that, by the third generation, there's a portfolio of enterprises within the family company. Having multiple enterprises raises such issues as "How do we make decisions about allocation of capital?" "How do we make decisions about what is adequate or appropriate or excellent performance in the various parts of our company?" and "How do we take action on those parts of our company where the family members running them are underperforming or are superstars? If they are superstars, should they be rewarded more amply than other family members? Would that be seen as unfair?"

> . . . a Cousin Collaboration is in partnership with the board and management in planning a strategy that meets the needs of both business and family.

The cousins may or may not be people who are trained, skilled, or experienced in dealing with strategic questions. If not, some mechanism has to be developed on behalf of ownership to deal with the question of strategy. Generally, top management should be developing and recommending strategy to the board of directors. Management should have a solid understanding of the goals and values of the family and the strategy it recommends should be consistent with those goals and values. The board, which represents ownership, endorses proposed strategies, provides oversight of management, and reports to ownership. Ownership may want to reserve some decisions, such as to sell the company or for make a significant acquisition, for a vote of the entire ownership group.

Essentially, a Cousin Collaboration is in partnership with the board and management in planning a strategy that meets the needs of both business and family.

Family owners should provide parameters for management's development of strategy and the board's oversight of the company's direction. These parameters relate to owners' collective goals relating to growth, risk, rate of return, and liquidity.

One way the cousins can strengthen their strategic capabilities is to include on the board executives from other companies with proven strategic experience. Such outsiders can provide invaluable perspectives about strategic planning to less experienced family board members and other owners.

Other ways to shore up strategic-planning knowledge and skills are to include educational programs on the topic at family or shareholders' meetings, hire a consultant to work with the Cousin Collaboration on its role in strategic planning, and read books and articles that deal with the subject. We make some suggestions for further reading at the end of this book.

Keep in mind that what's going on in the family strongly influences business strategy and vice versa. Whether or not there are family members in the business capable of leading a particular strategy may determine whether or not that strategy is selected. Alternatively, a family may be open to having non-family executives lead if the strategy seems right.

LEADERSHIP

As the last paragraph suggests, much attention must be devoted to the issue of business leadership. The cousins will find that many leadership-related questions need to be discussed. Is there enough motivated, committed talent in the cousin group to provide effective leadership, in the top positions? If not, can such talent be developed? Or, should non-family leaders fill in until family leadership is available?

Should some positions, such as CEO and chairman, be reserved for family members? Or should the cousins turn these positions over to non-family executives? If that's the choice, the cousins may want to revisit the question, "Do we want to continue owning this business together and, if so, why?"

If the cousins prefer that the business be led at the top levels by family members, it is important that they honestly assess whether there is sufficient ability within the family to fill the key positions. They must also commit themselves to recruiting and developing the most talented family members for those leadership roles.

As we have indicated earlier, a family business increasingly relies on having non-family executives fill key positions by the cousin generation, as the business becomes larger and relatively fewer family members join the company. Many business-owning families decide that they want to fill their companies' top executive positions with the best people, regardless of whether or not they are family members. They believe such a decision will assure the continuity of a great legacy that they want to pass on to their children. And if there is no family member in the top roles in the current generation, they don't rule out the possibility that terrific business leaders might emerge in the next generation of family members.

Whether they realize it or not, some families stack the deck in favor of family members winning the leadership spots. That's not necessarily good for the business or the family. Cousin-owners should guard against making it easy for family members to hold positions of high responsibility. Family members are less likely to develop their full leadership potential unless they are subjected to the same rigors that everybody else vying for a top position would face. What's more, such family members will be perceived as having been unduly favored and will have a more difficult time gaining respect when they hold leadership positions.

Highlights for Children, Inc., has a non-family president, Elmer Meider, who has been employed in the company for nearly 20 years. It's important, he suggests, to have family members involved in the business but to recognize that nepotism can create problems.

At Highlights, he says, "family members will not be promoted unless they are equal to or more qualified than non-family members. I can honestly say, as a non-family executive, they [the family] have held very dear to that during my 19 years with the company.

"I do believe that a family business will fail if they don't follow that rule. Two things can go wrong: one, you have an unqualified person doing the job; and two, the qualified person decides it doesn't matter and leaves. So you get a double whammy."[8]

Business leadership also encompasses the board of directors. If the sibling generation has not presented the cousins with an effective board, the cousins may have some cleaning up to do. In our work with family firms, we sometimes find boards with too many people on them, or too many family members, most of whom make little contribution. Too often, boards are organized along branch lines, with an equal number of members representing each branch. They are looking out after their own nuclear families, not the family as a whole and not the business. No wonder, then, that good decisions are so hard to make and the board is unable to provide satisfactory guidance to management.

Family members on well-functioning boards represent the best interests of the total family and the business.

Generally, boards are most effective when there are four to seven members, with a majority of the slots (or a significant minority) reserved for experienced, objective, and knowledgeable outsiders, such as CEOs of other companies. Family members on well-functioning boards represent the best interests of the total family and the business.

FAMILY EMPLOYMENT

An extension of the leadership discussion is the matter of family employment. If the preceding generation had a family employment policy, it's time for the cousins to review it and determine if it is still viable. Where the business was probably able to absorb all the members of the sibling generation, it is neither likely nor desirable that it can provide employment to all the cousins unless they are a small group. New standards and rules for entry into the business will need to be developed to fit the new circumstances.

The question is, "What will the family' role in the business be going forward?" Suppose the cousins have determined that there are, at least in their generation, no family members who can fill the top-tier paid leadership roles? The next question is, "Should opportunities be made available to family members commensurate with their skills and their ambitions at any level in the company?" Some family members, after all, will be happy to work in lesser leadership positions and they can, in fact, make valuable contributions. Think of engineers, mechanics, artists, writers, scientists, computer whizzes, and the like who are experts in their fields but who don't want or don't have the talent to be managers.

As one group of cousins put it, however, "We don't want to become the employer of last resort. We don't want to give a family member a job just because she 'needs' it. Family members have to bring something to the table."

Some families have to grapple with the issue of disabled family members and whether or not jobs should be made available to them. Stephen Marriott, one of the sons of J. W. "Bill" Marriott Jr., the long-time CEO of Marriott International, Inc., is blind and nearly deaf as a result of a rare disease. Still, he earned an M.B.A. and worked his way up to vice president of labor in the family-controlled firm.

Nevertheless, Bill Marriott told the *Wall Street Journal*, Stephen "understands that because of his disabilities, there's not much more he can do."[9] In other words, while successful at his current level, it was not expected that Stephen would ever rise to the CEO level.

We see different cousin groups making a variety of decisions about family employment. They look something like this:

EXHIBIT 6   **Family Employment and Leadership Spectrum**

- ◆ All family members are welcome to work in the business, no matter what.
- ◆ Only family members who have specified qualifications (education, experience, etc.) are welcome to work in the
Continued

> business, and only if there are positions available that
> match their abilities. (Family members with special needs
> will be considered on a case-by-case basis.)
> ◆ No family members will work in the business. We want
>   employment and leadership decisions to be driven purely
>   by what's best for the business.
> ◆ Top leadership positions are reserved for family members.
> ◆ Top leadership positions are open to the best candidates,
>   whether family members or not. Our commitment as
>   cousins is to be effective owners. We're about overseeing
>   the business but we're not about running the business.
> ◆ If there are no family members running the business,
>   there's no reason to continue to own the business.

COMPENSATION

An important part of making a family firm more professional is
to change the compensation policy to one that is more reflective
of market-based compensation practices employed in non-family
companies. Siblings who work in the business often get paid the
same. But equal pay for family members is unlikely to be a successful compensation system in the cousin generation.

The Cousin Collaboration should look at what kinds of financial contributions are being generated by different profit centers within the family business. It should develop an appropriate
approach to bonuses and incentive pay that is based primarily on
what's actually happening in the business as opposed to membership in the owning family.

The cousins may create or revise an overall compensation
policy to convey through the board to management that base
pay is reflective of market rates, and that bonuses and incentive
pay are tied to performance, profitability, and the contribution
that an individual makes to an enterprise. The policy should also
take into account the need to reward the non-family managers
appropriately.

MANAGING EXPECTATIONS

The five sibling owners of a regional food specialty chain we'll call Giordano Family Markets have been working hard to set the stage for the cousin generation. One of the ways they are doing this is by establishing expectations for the family and for the business.

They have all agreed that they want to have a family member leading the company. To realize that goal, they have set an expectation for themselves. "We're going to be proactive about encouraging talented family members to join the business and developing them to lead it," said Jerry, the current CEO. They have also begun to develop policies and practices that will spell out to all family members what the expectations are for the business and for the family. For example, an employment policy makes it clear to the 17 cousins—all still in their teens—what is expected of them if they wish to seek employment and advance in the family's $60 million company.

The siblings make up the board of directors, but they are taking steps to create a more professional, objective board. One brother and one sister have volunteered to resign from the board to make room for some outside directors, and the sibling team is looking for potential directors who can best help them take their company to the next level but who also understand family businesses. "For one thing, we want our children to understand that not every family member can or ought to be on the board," said Anne, the sister who will resign. "We also want to serve as models of owners who can all work together effectively even though some of us may not be in the business or on the board."

Once the new board is in place, a committee will work on developing a compensation policy that is more appropriate for their growing company. When appropriate, the policy will be shared with the next generation so that they understand how they will be rewarded if they are employed in the company.

The siblings have also asked a consultant and their attorney to help them in creating a buy–sell agreement that will clarify issues of liquidity. The Giordanos want to help current and future owners and spouses understand under what circumstances they can sell their shares and what the financial expectations and consequences might be if they do. They are also beginning work on a dividend policy that will be more appropriate to a business with a larger number of shareholders. They haven't decided on all the details yet, but they believe dividends should be linked to profits and performance.

In addition, the siblings, who are in their 40s and 50s, are disciplining themselves to be clearer about their financial expectations for the business. They know that such clarity will be even more important in the next generation of owners, when there will be more owners outside the business than in it and when the family will be more dispersed. They are aiming at being knowledgeable enough to state such expectations to their new board as, "We hope to be growing at x percent," or "We don't want our debt to be more than x percent of equity," or whatever measures they determine. If they can do that, they again will serve as a model for their children—not only in setting expectations for the business but also in helping ownership understand what expectations are desirable and reasonable and in keeping with the family's values.

The siblings have formed a family council that includes some of the spouses in committee leadership roles. One of the wives is heading up an education committee. She is looking at ways to educate family members, including spouses and future owners, about how family businesses work, finance, and effective ownership. She's planning to create some special programs for the cousins at family retreats—to help them see what a wonderful legacy Giordano Family Markets is and to help them understand that they have an important role in the company's future.

... when expectations are intelligently defined and the family is educated, necessary changes can be more readily embraced.

The Giordano siblings know that the advent of the cousin generation requires many changes in the way a business is managed. Unless expectations are understood, some of those changes can be unduly painful—separating some family members from board membership, for example, or rejecting some family members who might want to work in the business. Or family members can develop inappropriate expectations—feeling entitled to a seat on the board, for example, or to compensation equal to another family member working in the company, or to a higher dividend.

But when expectations are intelligently defined and the family is educated, necessary changes can be more readily embraced.

Chapter 7

The Art of Governance
in a Cousin Business

Family business succession is an often misunderstood concept. Many think of it as simply passing the top executive slot from one person to another at a certain point in time. But it's much more extensive and complex than that. Among other things, **succession involves preparing the entire family business governance system for continuity.** It's about the design of the board of directors and the leadership of the board, the chair role. And it's about evolution in how decisions are made. Rather than being an event that transpires in the space of time it takes to change the nameplate on an office door, it is a dynamic, ongoing process that happens over a period of years.

What makes succession in the governance system so difficult, as the ownership moves from a smaller group of siblings to a larger group of cousins, is that the basic assumptions about governance change dramatically. We call this "The Great Governance Transformation." Consider the exhibit on page 62, which describes governance under the two different circumstances. The exhibit will seem somewhat familiar to you because of transitions between the sibling generation and the cousin generation that we have examined previously. You might even want to compare it to Exhibit 1, "How Conditions Change," on page 9. The main difference here is that you can now think of these transitions as changes taking place not just in the family

EXHIBIT 7   Governance Transitions

	Sibling Partnership	Cousin Collaboration
Positions	Partitioned among family members so each has own turf	Open for any qualified person
Involvement	Everyone has a role; all or most senior roles taken by family members	Not everyone is interested or qualified for a role; some roles are taken by highly qualified independent outsiders
Representation	Each branch is represented in governance and decision making	All positions are "at large" positions regardless of branch politics or preferences
Preparation	On the job, after the fact	A program run by the family council before selected to governance roles
Evaluation	If any, very informal and based on work style	Formal system based on merit and results
Compensation	Presumed equal; variations based on negotiations among siblings	Merit system based on external market data
Family Leadership	Ill-defined; informal	Defined positions and formal selection
Decision Making	Consensus	Democracy— including outsiders (non-family)

or the business but in the overall family business governance system.

In short, the governance system converts from an informal one led by a team of owner-operators to a formal one led by family governors. If the business does not yet have a board with independent outsiders, the Cousin Collaboration should give very serious thought to developing one. Other structures should also be put in place if they do not yet exist—a family council and an ownership group, for example.

Given the complexity of the changes we are discussing, the transition will likely require an external change agent and other resources to educate the family on the nature of the transformation and to help it overcome potential resistance. Those resources include a consultant, an independent director or two, a member of the business (e.g., the human resources director), a business advisor (like a lawyer), representatives of a family business that has made the governance transition successfully, or one or two members of the family with no expected role in the new governance system.

TRICKY ISSUES

The great governance transition of the cousin stage requires the family to make decisions about a host of difficult topics. Here are some of them. As you go through them, remember that in the cousin stage, there are many family owners, and most likely more family owners than there are family members working in the company.

1. What Kind of Board(s) Do We Want?

a. Support or accountability? When you bring independent outsiders onto your business board of directors, do you want people who truly understand, appreciate, empathize with, and are sympathetic to the particular issues and attitudes of a family company that is a cousin-owned business and that is being held for the long term? Most likely, such independents will come from family businesses themselves or have a strong family business background. They empathize with and provide support in relation to family dynamics and issues.

Or do you want people who will bring a different perspective and push the organization to be more disciplined? They might come from public companies or financial disciplines. They will challenge some of the fundamental assumptions of the family business. For example, they may not accept the notion that you should compromise shareholder value in the short term to build long-term stability and value as you deal with family dynamics. "I don't care if he's your nephew," they might say. "If he isn't doing what needs to be done to fix that division, he needs to be replaced now. The family will just have to deal with it." Or as another public company CEO serving as a director of a family business put it, "You just identify the problem and figure out how to solve it. Why are we talking about all this family stuff?" Such directors focus on accountability.

Directors who stress business accountability might make you a bit uncomfortable but they can be stimulating and inject creativity. You may be more comfortable with supportive outsiders, but because they are so like you, they won't offer as wide a range of valuably different perspectives. Supportive directors are more likely to allow you to convince yourself that the business compromises that you make in the name of family peace are all right.

Consider this: Would a combination of sympathetic and cantankerous outsiders be the best answer for your board?

b. Independents on other family boards. If you're a larger family business, you should consider whether you want independent outsiders on your family council board, your family foundation board, your family office board, and so on. Families that own businesses with subsidiaries also need to make decisions about how independent the subsidiary boards should be from one another and what kinds of outsiders they should have.

2. Who Is "Family"?

By the cousin stage, this already complicated issue becomes even more complicated. When you have a family activity, who's included? What age are the children when they are invited to participate? Are spouses included? Do they, for example, have a vote about where the next family meeting will be? Who gets to vote for officers of the family council? What about stepchildren? Or ex-spouses (the parents of children who are part of the family bloodline, after all)?

Another question that arises is, "What about family members who have sold their shares?" Often, they "disappear," but not always. And it's not necessarily desirable for them to withdraw from the family organization. They may have a lot to offer and a lot of energy to give.

So what's "typical" in terms of "who's family?" may not be right for your family.

3. How Are Family Members Selected for Governance Roles?

That is, how do you pick family members for the business board, the family council, or, if you have one, the family foundation board or the family office board?

a. Merit or representation? Do you choose family members who you feel need exposure to the boards? Do you more or less rotate different family members through so they can learn and gain ease with a governing environment? Or should you select family members who have the best qualifications for the position? Again, is a combination of the two approaches a possible solution?

b. Limited terms? If it's truly a merit system, do you leave the terms unlimited so that the most qualified person stays on the board indefinitely? Or do you say, "We're going to use a merit system but we're going to have limits on it. You can serve no more than three three-year terms"? On one hand, unlimited terms enable you to benefit indefinitely from the wisdom and experience of committed, knowledgeable, and caring family members. On the other hand, term limits permit you to assess various talents and ease out a family member who may not have lived up to expectations without inflicting the pain of judgment. ("Sorry! Your term is up, and we're not allowed to re-elect you.")

c. **Slate or compete?** Do you appoint a nominating committee to recruit and/or screen family members and present the most qualified as a slate? Or, do you have entirely competitive elections, saying, "We have three openings and six people who are interested. Pick your three favorites."

Typically, family businesses decide they want to avoid open competition. They go the slate route and include, in the process, the opportunity for competition. The recommended candidates are presented on the slate, but if someone else wants to compete, he or she can be nominated from the floor, self-nominate, or create a write-in campaign.

d. **Open or secret?** Do people vote on a secret ballot or do they vote by a show of hands? A show of hands may be fine for a slate, but a secret ballot is more appropriate and desirable when there's open competition.

e. **Evaluating family.** Suppose you have a merit system, or suppose you have a representative system with three-year terms and a limit of nine years altogether? How do you evaluate people in their roles? Do you have a formal evaluation process? Does the nominating committee ask family members how well Patrick is doing after his first three years on the family council? Does the family have a mechanism for giving feedback to family members so that, if necessary, they can make improvements? How do family members in official roles know whether or not they are perceived as doing a good job? Some families have regular evaluation processes. (One example would be a regular survey of shareholders asking for feedback about family members who are on the company board of directors.)

The danger of an open competition for voting and of an evaluation system is that when someone is not elected initially or not re-elected, bitterness or disaffection can result. Family members may not serve rather than risk losing. Those who don't win may then lose interest in the business or the family. "To heck with this," they say. "I'm not going to try again." It can be a very sensitive issue.

4. Who Selects Governance?

a. Who should be on the nominating committee? Should you have one nominating committee for all of your structures (boards, family council, etc.) or should there be a separate nominating committee for each? Should you have a separate governance committee that manages governance for the entire system? Should the nominating committee be the family council? Or should it be a composite of some of the business board members plus family at large?

b. Per capita or per share? As mentioned in Chapter 5, how you count the votes is one of the special challenges that cousin businesses face. Board and ownership decisions legally require per share votes, but family decisions can be made on a per person vote. For a full discussion of this issue, please return to page 45.

c. Defining "fair process" for the first time. Another special issue we talked about in Chapter 5 was how to introduce democracy in a fair way. Doing so requires defining what a fair process is even before you begin. It's almost a "chicken-or-egg" situation, for to have democracy, you need to have a fair process, but to agree on what a fair process is, you need a fair way to define it! Like most families faced with this issue, you'll muddle through until you arrive at the point where your democracy works reasonably smoothly.

Remember, however, that in a democracy, there will be some winners and some losers, and what people really need to feel is that the system by which decisions are made is just. There are many ingredients that go into fair process. It is transparent—everyone knows what's going on. There are no hidden agendas. People don't have conflicts of interest. People know the rules before they get involved. The rules stay as consistent as possible. And there's a chance to review the rules from time to time and make corrections or modifications.

Scott Family Enterprises stumbled over a fairness issue several years ago. The Scotts own two major businesses—First Interstate BancSystem, Inc. (FIBS), based in Billings, Montana, and Padlock Ranch, a substantial cow-calf operation headquartered in north central Wyoming.

Discord and disappointment resulted when the five siblings in the second generation ignored agreed-upon guidelines for nominating and selecting candidates for the FIBS board. Instead of nominating two third-generation candidates as originally planned, the siblings decided to expand the number of board positions and recommended three candidates, whose nominations were subsequently ratified by the Scott Family Council. Some of the siblings weren't officially part of the nominations process but they sat in as "observers" and, in effect, influenced the outcome.

Some family members were concerned that the second generation had been motivated for reasons of family branch representation.

"The five of them would get together and make the decisions. That's the way it has always been," said a third-generation cousin. "It seems like we take two steps forward and one step back."[10]

In a letter to the family council, another cousin said that "it pains me to see how the latest election process and the actions of the 2nd generation will surely fragment our family further."[11]

The Scotts have been working hard to repair the damage. With the aid of outside consultants, they have developed the following guidelines to promote fairness in family decisions:

EXHIBIT 8   Scott Family Fair Process Guidelines

- ◆ No surprises—everyone knows the issue and the call to decision beforehand.
- ◆ No conflicts of interest—personal interest and agendas are disclosed.

- No rush—everyone feels that they have time to prepare and time to present their views.
- Sincere care—each participant feels respected and heard.
- Mutual commitment—genuine effort is made to find a "win-win" solution before a vote or decision.
- Good conduct—if proceedings were videotaped and shown to future generations, the process is a good example of which all would be proud.
- Objective outsiders—independent directors or family facilitators represent the interests of everyone, not some.
- Post-decision review—everyone discusses their views of the process and agrees to review the results of the decision later.

Source: "Scott Family Enterprises (Part B): Addressing Family Goals and Visions in the Family Enterprise," a case study prepared by Canh Tran and John L. Ward. Copyright 2004 by the J. L. Kellogg School of Management, Northwestern University, Evanston, IL.

5. Employing, Compensating, and Providing Incentives to Family

It's a given that family members who work in the business get paid for doing so. Those who work in the business also receive bonuses, benefits, and perks. Those serving as board members may receive director's fees like independent outside directors who receive a board fee for their service and in some cases earn incentives based on the company's performance, such as stock options or bonuses. One question that arises is whether family members on the board participate in those incentives as well. If they do, how will that change their alignment with respect to the interests of the rest of the family? Other family members may say, "Our view is long, long term, but if you receive an incentive as a family member on the board, you may focus on short-term decisions to earn the incentive."

In the cousin generation, multiple governing
bodies begin.

As your family gets larger and your scope of family activities
gets wider, additional issues come to the table. In the cousin generation, multiple governing bodies begin. As a result, you now have
a number of family members who are not working in the company
but who are playing important, time-consuming roles in service to
the family. You may have a family council, to which family members volunteer their time. But if the family is large and wealthy
enough, you may also have a family foundation, a family office, or
a family investment company—all of which require professional
management. Do you want family members to be employed in
these entities? Will family members working in the family office
have access to confidential information about other family members that is not available to all? Will providing incentives to family employees give them a financial advantage over other family
members? The boards of these organizations are probably going
to include family members. Should they receive compensation?

6. Funding Family Interests

Funds will be needed to support such family activities as a family
council, an annual reunion, or a newsletter. The family may create a family office for members' use. Perhaps the office includes
some support staff to provide assistance to family members. How
will you pay for all of that?

Here are some options:

a. Generational gift. The members of the older generation
pay for some or all of it, as a gift. "We think this family stuff is
important," they say. "We've accumulated more wealth because
we're older. We've got young people in the family who would
find it a hardship to fly to Hawaii for a family reunion. So we, the
seniors, will pick up the tab."

b. Endowment. The older generation or perhaps the family
as a whole endows the costs. Suppose the family's activities cost

$100,000 a year. It sets aside $2 million for an endowment fund that returns 5 percent—or $100,000—annually. The returns are used to pay for the activities. No one ever has to raise money for them again and no family members have to be billed for their participation.

A variation is to set aside sufficient company stock for the endowment fund. The shares (sometimes a separate class of preferred stock) are held by the family as a group (often in a trust) and the dividends are used for family activities.

c. Use. Everyone pays personally for whatever services they use. If they go to the family reunion, they pay their own way. The downside is that younger family members with less means may not go to family reunions or participate in other ways. Individual parents often help here or limited family or business funds may be made available to help family members of lesser means.

7. Keeping Family and Governance Close

How can a Cousin Collaboration keep members of a widespread, diverse family close to the action and feeling like they're on the "big team"? One way is to invite them to be observers of governance activities. Perhaps only three family members sit on the business's board of directors and five others are running the family council, but the meetings are open and other family members are encouraged to attend as observers. Even foundation board meetings could sometimes be open.

Depending on the size of the family or on its culture, some restrictions may apply. If you need to limit the number of observers who can attend at any one time, you might institute a rotating, rationed system. ("At this meeting, the first three people who call can attend. At the next meeting, the first three people who call can come unless you came last time.") You may need to set some ground rules to limit commotion. ("No side conversations and no cell phones, please.") And, you'll need to educate observers so that they understand that if the board goes into executive session, they will have to leave the room.

Another way to keep family close to governance is to have informal, informational sessions where a board or the council meets with the family for lunch or after the board meeting. Once a year, perhaps, there might be a joint meeting of the business or foundation board and the family as a whole. Familywide "town hall" meetings can be useful in helping family councils understand the concerns and wishes of family members on specific issues.

Good information and good interaction are really helpful in building trust in a system of representative democracy.

Some questions that the cousins need to discuss include: What information do we pass out? Do we send the minutes to the family as a whole or put reports in the newsletter about what's happening in the various governance bodies? Sending out minutes of board meetings is tricky because family members start getting concerned about how widely information is being distributed and whether confidentiality or security is being breached. On the other hand, reports in newsletters can seem "official" when they are not, or create other misunderstandings unless carefully worded.

The goal is to keep the family and the governance system confident in each other, comfortable, trusting, and close. Good information and good interaction are really helpful in building trust in a system of representative democracy.

8. Clarifying Roles and Responsibilities of Owners

Sometimes owners have difficulty sorting out what their role is. If you are an owner in a larger, cousin-stage business and you have no other responsibilities, just what is it that you do?

We would argue that the owners as a group are responsible for shaping values, vision, goals, and policies. Owners need to provide guidance to the board on such questions as: Where are we going? How much do we want to grow? How much do we want to be diversified? What do we look for from the company

that we own? Owners also need to develop family business policies ranging from such topics as rules for family members working in the business to prenuptial contracts and qualifications for
board membership.

Owners need a venue in which to come together to express
their views. Oftentimes, it's the family council. Some families,
however, prefer to separate the family council, which is based on
family membership, from the owners' group, which is based on
share ownership.

Owners need a venue in which to come together
to express their views.

An important question for ownership, particularly as the family gets larger and more democratic, is: Will the family speak
with one voice or will it present a diversity of views? When the
family speaks to the board of the business, will it give a single
guidance or will it present a divided guidance? Will it say, "This
is our collective judgment. You now have a clear direction from
us"? Or will the family say, "We discussed this matter a lot and
62 percent of the family thought this but 38 percent thought
that. So you need to know that there is a significant minority
opinion on this issue"?

If the family speaks with one voice, the board knows exactly
what the family wants and needn't be concerned that the family
is disagreeing or is in danger of breaking up. Nor does it have
to worry about favoring some family members and not others.
The disadvantage of one voice is that board members don't really
know the diversity of opinion within the family and can't factor
that into their judgments.

Generally what we find is that until a family gains confidence
that a divided view is not going to break it up, speaking with
one voice makes the most sense. When people are confident that
they will stay together win or lose, then having diverse voices is
possible and even desirable.

9. Addressing Role Conflicts

The smaller the family, the more likely you are to experience role conflicts because you're more likely to have people playing multiple roles. Joe is an owner, the CEO, and chairman of the board. His sister, Eleanor, is an owner, a vice president of the business, a member of the board, and the chairperson of the family council. Sometimes what Joe wants as CEO is at odds with what he wants as a family member. Sometimes the views that Eleanor has as the leader of the family don't jibe with what she thinks is best for the business in her job as vice president.

Role conflicts occur in larger family businesses as well, and don't involve just family members but also trustees, advisors, and directors. If someone is the company's legal advisor, can he or should he also be a trustee of a family member's estate. Can he also be on the board?

In a perfect world, we'd say, "Avoid conflicts of interest." As a practical matter, however, sometimes people with conflicts of interest are the best people for the roles they play. What's important is that everybody understand what the conflicts are.

10. Providing Amendability to Family Agreements

How easy or difficult is it to change major documents, such as a shareholders' agreement or a family constitution (a compilation of the family's mission and values statements and family business policies)? If it is too easy to change them, then they don't have a whole lot of meaning. If it is too hard to revise them, they can become unsuitable to changing circumstances.

We've seen cases where families have made some pieces of their constitutions unchangeable—such as trusts that must make decisions according to specified rules. Unalterability creates a sense of consistency and stability. Family ambiguity, however, can lead to family conflict, which, in turn, can result in big problems.

But when agreements can't be revised and improved, family members feel disenfranchised and resentful. They lose interest, and the agreements themselves become unworkable because they are so irrelevant to the times.

Some families regularly review these documents every five years. Others review their documents thoroughly with every generational transition.

MAKING TRADE-OFFS

Exhibit 9 offers another way to look at the governance decisions and suggests some of the trade-offs families make when they lean in one direction or another:

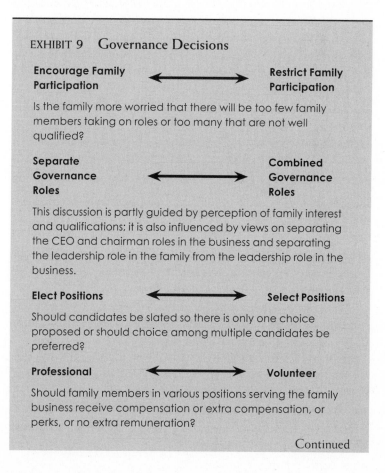

EXHIBIT 9   Governance Decisions

Encourage Family Participation ←——————→ **Restrict Family Participation**

Is the family more worried that there will be too few family members taking on roles or too many that are not well qualified?

Separate Governance Roles ←——————→ **Combined Governance Roles**

This discussion is partly guided by perception of family interest and qualifications; it is also influenced by views on separating the CEO and chairman roles in the business and separating the leadership role in the family from the leadership role in the business.

Elect Positions ←——————→ **Select Positions**

Should candidates be slated so there is only one choice proposed or should choice among multiple candidates be preferred?

Professional ←——————→ **Volunteer**

Should family members in various positions serving the family business receive compensation or extra compensation, or perks, or no extra remuneration?

Continued

Rotation 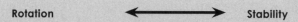 **Stability**

Is it preferred that roles rotate among family members or that effective incumbents remain in position for an indefinite period of time?

Larger Board  **Smaller Board**

A larger board/council/committee allows more participation. Smaller boards/councils/committees improve group effectiveness.

Insiders on Board  **Outsiders on Board**

The mix of family and non-family is a decision that requires careful consideration.

Prequalified Capabilities  **On-the-Job Training**

Should people prove themselves before they serve or have the opportunity to learn on the job? The family can also consider subsidiary boards, family committee participation, and junior (shadow) boards for development.

Statutory Cross Fertilization  **Each Board Independent**

If your family has multiple companies, will each board be independent of all other boards? Or will family members serve on several business and family boards? The former creates more opportunities for people to be involved while the latter allows for a greater exchange of ideas among the entities and for more monitoring of the performance of each enterprise.

PHILANTHROPIC ISSUES

If the family wishes to engage in joint philanthropic activities, governance issues with respect to those matters must also be resolved. If a family foundation already exists, it might become increasingly professional and defined. During the sibling stage, a family foundation is typically a family vehicle for charitable giving and only a few people have influence over it. Decisions are made by consensus or the siblings divide up the funds and each makes decisions about his or her portion. This approach is rarely practical in the cousin generation. Now, as with everything else, decision making becomes more democratic and a board may be appointed that includes knowledgeable outsiders as well as family members.

The family should still provide guidance, however, and the Cousin Collaboration will need to discuss these questions:

1. What's the purpose of the family's philanthropic efforts? In the early stages, the family's philanthropy was primarily an expression of the charitable interests of the siblings or the founding parents. Now, most likely, the cousins will want to shift the mission. Instead of giving a little bit of money to each individual's favorite charities, the family may wish to increase the impact of its philanthropic contributions by seeking to be more strategic, giving substantial funds to a collective family interest in order to make a real difference.

In the sibling generation, a family fund or foundation may have given modest amounts to a plethora of community organizations. Now, however, some family members want to give to Planned Parenthood while others want to support right-to-life groups, and some want to support the arts while others think doing so is wasteful.

Because of this diversity, larger families find themselves looking for a common focus, and what they might say is, "Any family member can give anything they want to out of their own personal money, but the family's charitable funds will focus on buying property in our community to preserve for parks." Or they might decide that funds should be targeted to research on workplace safety or providing scholarships to the children of the family firm's employees. Thus family members have the freedom to support their favorite causes individually plus the opportunity to make a greater impact with collective funds.

2. What is the role of the family? The cousins will have to decide how to make philanthropic decisions. If the family has a foundation, will family members sit on the board or will any of them actually work in the foundation? Will other people be asked to evaluate the proposals that come in or will family members appraise the submissions themselves? When family members do the evaluations, they become more engaged and philanthropic work becomes more personal to them. But they also run the risk of disagreeing with one another about what to support, and the process of evaluating numerous proposals can absorb an enormous amount of time. Several successful entrepreneurs have observed that it is harder to give money away responsibly than it is to earn it in the first place.

The cousins will have to decide how to make philanthropic decisions.

While working together on philanthropic matters poses some governance challenges, doing so offers some desirable side benefits. **It gives the family another opportunity to demonstrate its values, and it helps family members bond with one another through their involvement in a significant purpose.**

PREPARING FAMILY MEMBERS
FOR GOVERNANCE

Just as the incumbent generation provides career development opportunities in the family business for members of the next generation, so must it prepare them for governance roles in both the business and the family. The family might create a "shadow" business board, family council, or ownership council, in which teenage family members can get practice discussing and making decisions about issues they will face as adults. They might even be invited to make some input into the real family council.

College-age and older family members can be given opportunities to observe business or foundation board meetings. The
family can also provide training sessions in which board or council members tell inexperienced family members what they do.

By the time they have reached their upper teens, young people
can begin to get some experience by serving on family committees, helping to plan a family retreat or newsletter, for example.
They can also be sent to leadership training sessions and family
business seminars offered by various university family business
centers. They can gain leadership exposure outside of the family
organization in school or other organizations.

Special courses at family retreats on such topics as decision
making, effective communication, making presentations, and
family business dynamics can help them develop strengths for
future governance responsibilities.

Don't forget adult family members. Some may be late bloom-
ers or may have career or family obligations that kept them from
active participation as young adults. But they may want to be
more involved later and will welcome opportunities to learn more
about the responsibilities of family business governance.

The more that people understand good governance and their
role in it, the greater chance there will be for harmony in the
family and success in the business.

Chapter 8

Assuring Continuity and Success

A healthy family is the foundation of continued success in a cousin-owned business. By "healthy family," we mean one where relationships are respectful and friendly, communication is good, and conflicts are prevented or dealt with satisfactorily. All of us know of family businesses that have crumbled because the owning family fell apart.

A healthy family is the foundation of continued success in a cousin-owned business.

We believe observing the following five principles will help the Cousin Collaboration achieve and sustain the health of the family so that the family, in turn, can support and sustain the business:

1. THE CENTER OF THE FAMILY IS THE FAMILY

In the sibling era, the business may often be the glue that holds the family together. The business is central to family members' lives. It is the focus of their energies and the source of their live-lihood, and commitment to it and hours spent in it are often seen as measures of one's worth. Lack of commitment to the business may be perceived as lack of commitment to the family. Or people may feel that if they don't work in the business, they won't be seen as full-fledged family members.

Wise cousin groups shift the focus from the business to the family and create other means for fostering unity, such as family councils, family social events, or family philanthropy. Remember the Scott family, which you met in Chapter 7? To get to know each other better, the 19 Scott cousins and their spouses got together for a social gathering in 1993 and have had a yearly social event ever since. They also hold a "cousin" camp at the family's Padlock Ranch in the summer.

2. A SENSE OF PURPOSE KEEPS COUSINS TOGETHER

What really unifies the cousins and secures their commitment to the business more than anything else is that they believe the business fulfills a social purpose. The business is not just an eco-nomic asset but an emotional one. The cousins are excited by the opportunity to participate in something larger and more impor-tant than themselves and are often willing to sacrifice econom-ically in order to have that privilege. Susan Dryfoos, one of the 13 members of the highly united cousin group in the Sulzberger family, speaks of the *New York Times* as "a trust" and "a tradition that is far greater than any single individual."[12]

The business is not just an economic asset but an emotional one.

Like the Sulzberger cousins, many successful cousin groups view the family business as a legacy or an heirloom. They can't imagine selling the company because they fear a buyer would compromise its purpose. The Scott family, for example, looks at Padlock Ranch as a model of environmental stewardship and takes pride in how their banking company has played a positive role in the lives of their employees and in the communities in which the branches are located.

3. A DYNAMIC FAMILY COUNCIL AND A FAMILY CONSTITUTION SUPPORT THE FAMILY IN ALL OF ITS ASPECTS

A strong, well-functioning family council looks after the needs of the family and serves as a forum for communications and decision making. It works very hard to address family and continuity issues. While it mobilizes the family to support the business and to prepare family members for roles in the business and for responsible ownership, its focus is on the family and the individuals within it. In many ways, it acts as the linchpin between family and business.

A strong, well-functioning family council looks after the needs of the family and serves as a forum for communications and decision making.

A family constitution brings together all the documents that guide the family, the business, and ownership. Such documents can include but are not limited to mission and values statements, policies, codes of conduct, and shareholder agreements. (Please see *The Family Constitution: Agreements to Secure and Perpetuate Your Family and Your Business.*)

4. BALANCING AND MANAGING "VOICE" AND "EXIT" ARE ESSENTIAL

This is one of the most critical concerns of cousin stage businesses. With the cousin generation come more owners of the family business than ever before and possibly the greater likelihood for dissatisfaction and dissent. Generally, it is better for a family business to retain its owners and not have to face the uncertainty or difficulty of having to buy back shares as a result of shareholder dissatisfaction or other reasons.

As noted in Chapter 5, "exit" here is concerned with the departure of a dissatisfied owner, while "voice" is the influence an owner can put forth to rectify the cause of dissatisfaction instead of exiting. Family shareholders usually find exiting ownership both emotionally difficult and financially disadvantageous. They may also feel a moral commitment to fix the problem they perceive rather than flee it. Family shareholders also have greater incentives—time, money, and emotion—to expand their effort to try to influence the business. After all, it may represent a large percentage of their net worth and of their personal identity.

Often family firms are encouraged to "protect the business first" by drafting buy–sell agreements that facilitate the exit of unhappy family owners or by working to assure that shareholders don't interfere with management.

While these are useful measures, too much reliance on them suffocates and frustrates the ability of owners to express their voice and influence things. If family owners feel that the exit options are unattractive but they are dissatisfied with the business's performance or conduct, then expressing voice is all they have (other than apathy and resignation).

We believe a balance between exit and voice is the solution. That means encouraging voice. Cousins can consider the ideas suggested below.

EXHIBIT 10 Six Ways to Encourage "Voice"

1. Provide opportunities for owners, directors, and managers to interact and share their views. Welcome the expression of concerns.
2. Include some family members on boards, along with a full complement of independent directors.
3. Survey shareholders anonymously from time to time. Let them know they were heard.
4. Educate family members to feel competent in expressing their opinions, both with business understanding and with communication skills.
5. Accept and respect dissenting views.
6. Promote a climate of trust and personal responsibility that keeps dissent constructive rather than destructive to management's capacity to manage.

Thinkers about exit and voice urge a continuation of both. Having one makes using the other more constructive and effective. If you as a family shareholder believe your voice will be respected, then you are less likely to exit. And, if access to exit is difficult, you will more likely try to use voice to reform things before choosing the irreversibility of exit.

Frequent discussion should take place in both the family and the boardroom about how well voice and exit are being managed. The balance between ease of exit and exercise of voice will probably shift from time to time. The capacity to make those shifts at artful moments is a critical element for family business continuity.

If you as a family shareholder believe your voice will be respected, then you are less likely to exit.

5. A "VALUES SYNERGY" SUPPORTS THE COUSINS' COMMITMENT TO BOTH FAMILY AND BUSINESS

Unlike their sibling parents, who focused on differences, savvy cousin-owners focus on values they can share. They know that concentrating on similarities, not dissimilarities, helps hold them together.

When family members see that the family's values are enhancing the business, their pride in those values and in the family gets reinforced. The family then realizes that the values it holds dear get extended through the business to the community. If the family members have a foundation or practice joint philanthropy in some other way, they also see how their values are embodied in the charitable work that they do.

In the cousin generation, each entity of the family builds on the others. The family council, with the support of the entire family, defines the values and transmits them to the ownership, the business, the family foundation, and so on. Cross-fertilization of each entity reinforces the values. The family gets positive feedback from employees, customers, vendors, and the community and understands that the values it believes in have made a positive difference on many levels. With such reinforcement, what family wouldn't feel closer?

Chapter 9

Summary

Despite the popular notion of "shirtsleeves to shirtsleeves in three generations," many cousin-generation businesses do succeed brilliantly. Yours can too. Doing so, however, requires a great deal of attention to the health of the family itself and a considerable amount of thought, discussion, and conscious decision making on the part of the cousins. We want to stress that word, *conscious*. Like every new generation in a family business, **cousins have the opportunity to review, renew, and revise. That's an opportunity that should not be squandered.**

The first and most critical questions cousins should discuss and resolve are: Do we want to continue owning this business together? If so, why? The decision to continue as partners should be intentional and not merely made out of inertia or because it's expected by one's parents or peers.

Once the cousins decide to move forward together, they need to forge themselves into a "Cousin Collaboration" that enables them to work as a team to reach agreed-upon goals. If they are successful, the family will thrive and the business will function like a dynamic democracy. The extended family will view itself as one family and its multiple businesses as one family enterprise. Family members will have trust in each other and the confidence to adapt their structures and processes to meet the needs of the time.

While it's desirable that family shareholders remain shareholders, they should have the opportunity to depart ownership without an emotional penalty. It will be up to the Cousin Collaboration to find ways to make continued ownership an attractive proposition. Family members who opt out should still be regarded as family members, not outcasts.

From this book, you have learned that the rules change when you go from siblings to cousins, just as they did when your business went from the founding generation to the siblings. And just as it was difficult for the founders to accept the changes when the siblings took over, so will it be difficult for the "sibs" to accept the changes that occur between their generation and that of their children. Fortunately, this is the last major transition a family business must make. Going from cousins to cousins is more like a public company making a transition from one system of leadership to the next. It should be less emotional and less stressful than the earlier family business transitions.

The cousins need to make new decisions about everything pertaining to the family and to the business, and they should not feel bound by what their parents thought and did. The world as the cousins know it is considerably different. That includes the business climate and the family itself, which has grown larger and much more diverse. The Cousin Collaboration increasingly professionalizes the business, hiring and promoting on merit, structuring performance appraisals, establishing greater accountability, and performing strategic planning.

Ideally, the sibling generation will understand that their children face a whole new world. The more the siblings set the stage for the cousins' success, the better. Siblings do this when they put policies and procedures in place that enable the cousins to trust one another and prepare them for leadership positions in both family and business. Siblings also set the stage when they initiate an understanding of family expectations—ranging from what standards must be met to join and advance in the family business to what the family wants from the business and what dividends are reasonable. If the siblings have not performed these tasks, the cousins will need to assume them.

> The family . . . is the foundation that helps make
> the business successful by defining the goals
> for which it should strive and the values that will
> guide its conduct.

Good, trustworthy, effective governance is essential. This implies not just governance of the business via a board of directors, but also governance of the family via such institutions as a family council, family office, or family philanthropic endeavor. Good governance not only offers assurances that all family members will be respectfully listened to but also provides opportunities for family members to participate in significant and critical ways both in the business and in the family. The family, after all, is the foundation that helps make the business successful by defining the goals for which it should strive and the values that will guide its conduct.

A strong, healthy family is essential to the success of a cousin-owned business. An effective family organization with good governance will not only strengthen the family, it will also strengthen the business. Basically, the challenge is more about the family than it is about the business—because without a united family, the business will be at risk.

When they set their hearts and minds to it, cousins can work together and give continuity to a viable business and the owning family. Transforming themselves from a disparate group of cousins who once hardly knew each other into a Cousin Collaboration will be both awe-inspiring and rewarding.

Notes

1. Thompson, Maria M., and Donald H. Price. *Wawa*. Charleston, SC: Arcadia Publishing, 2004, p. 8.
2. Goletz, Christina N. "Clemens Family Corporation (B): The Process of Change." Case study. Evanston, IL: J. L. Kellogg School of Management, Northwestern University, 2002, pp. 5–6.
3. Aronoff, Craig E. "Self-perpetuation Family Organization Built on Values: Necessary Condition for Long-term Family Business Survival." *Family Business Review*, Vol. 17, No. 1, March 2004, pp. 55–59.
4. Tifft, Susan E., and Alex S. Jones. *The Trust: The Private and Powerful Family Behind The New York Times*. Boston: Little, Brown and Co., 1999, p. 758.
5. Aronoff, Craig E., and John L. Ward. *Family Business Ownership: How to Be an Effective Shareholder*. Marietta, GA: Family Business Consulting Group/New York: Palgrave Macmillan, 2011, pp. 10–11.
6. Ibid., pp. 8–9.
7. Tomkies, Kelly Kagamas. "Highlights for Children, Inc. Survives the Challenge of an Unexpected Succession." *Family Business Advisor*, September 2005, pp. 5–6. Originally published as "All in the Family," *Smart Business Columbus* (http://columbus.sbnonline.com/), June 2005.
8. Ibid.
9. Binkley, Christina. "As Succession Looms, Marriott Ponders Keeping Job in Family." *Wall Street Journal*, May 19, 2005, pp. A1+.
10. Tran, Canh, and John L. Ward. "Scott Family Enterprises (Part A): Defining Fair Process for Cousin Owners." Case study. Evanston, IL: J. L. Kellogg School of Management, Northwestern University, 2004, p. 4.
11. Ibid., p. 2.
12. Tifft and Jones, *The Trust*, pp. 628–629.

Suggested Additional Readings

Aronoff, Craig E., Joseph H. Astrachan, Drew S. Mendoza, and John L. Ward. *Making Sibling Teams Work: The Next Generation.* Marietta, GA: Family Business Consulting Group/New York: Palgrave Macmillan, 2011.

Aronoff, Craig E., Joseph H. Astrachan, and John L. Ward. *Developing Family Business Policies: Your Guide to the Future.* Marietta, GA: Family Business Consulting Group/New York: Palgrave Macmillan, 2011.

Aronoff, Craig E., and Otis W. Baskin. *Effective Leadership in the Family Business.* Marietta, GA: Family Business Consulting Group/New York: Palgrave Macmillan, 2011.

Aronoff, Craig E., and John L. Ward. *Family Business Governance: Maximizing Family and Business Potential.* Marietta, GA: Family Business Consulting Group/New York: Palgrave Macmillan, 2011.

Aronoff, Craig E., and John L. Ward. *Family Business Values: How to Assure a Legacy of Continuity and Success.* Marietta, GA: Family Business Consulting Group/New York: Palgrave Macmillan, 2011.

Carlock, Randel S., and John L. Ward. *Strategic Planning for the Family Business: Parallel Planning to Unify the Family and Business.* New York: Palgrave, 2001.

de Visscher, Francois M., Craig E. Aronoff, and John L. Ward. *Financing Transitions: Managing Capital and Liquidity in Your Family Business.* Marietta, GA: Family Business Consulting Group/New York: Palgrave Macmillan, 2011.

"First Interstate BancSystem, Inc. Corporate Governance Guidelines." At https://www.firstinterstatebank.com/investor_relations/governance_guidelines.html.

Gersick, Kelin E., John A. Davis, Marion McCollom Hampton, and Ivan Lansberg. *Generation to Generation: Life Cycles of the Family Business.* Boston: Harvard Business School Press, 1997.

Lansberg, Ivan. *Succeeding Generations: Realizing the Dream of Families in Business.* Boston: Harvard Business School Press, 1999.

Montemerlo, Daniela, and John L. Ward. *The Family Constitution: Agreements to Secure and Perpetuate Your Family and Your Business.* Marietta, GA: Family Business Consulting Group/New York: Palgrave Macmillan, 2011.

Pendergast, Jennifer M., John L. Ward, and Stephanie Brun de Pontet. *Building a Successful Family Business Board: A Guide for Leaders, Directors, and Families.* Marietta, GA: Family Business Consulting Group/New York: Palgrave Macmillan, 2011.

Additional Sources

Ward, John L. "The Great Governance Transformation." Unpublished paper, 2001.

———. *Perpetuating the Family Business: 50 Lessons Learned from Long-Lasting, Successful Families in Business.* New York: Palgrave Macmillan, 2004.

———. "Voice and Exit in the Family Firm." Unpublished paper, 2002.

Index

The Authors

Craig E. Aronoff is Co-founder, Principal Consultant, and Chairman of the Board of the Family Business Consulting Group, Inc.; Founder of the Cox Family Enterprise Center; and current Professor Emeritus at Kennesaw State University. He invented and implemented the membership-based, professional-service-provider-sponsored Family Business Forum, which has served as a model of family business education for universities worldwide.

John L. Ward is Co-founder of the Family Business Consulting Group, Inc. He is Clinical Professor at the Kellogg School of Management and teaches strategic management, business leadership, and family enterprise continuity.

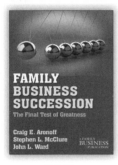

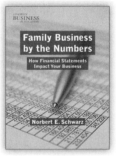